The Everlasting Sky

The Everlasting Sky

Voices of the Anishinabe People

GERALD VIZENOR

MINNESOTA HISTORICAL SOCIETY PRESS

Native Voices

Native peoples telling their stories, writing their history

To embody the principles set forth by the series, all Native Voices books are emblazoned with a bird glyph adapted from the Jeffers Petroglyph site in southern Minnesota. The rock art there represents one of the first recorded voices of Native Americans in the Upper Midwest. This symbol stands as a reminder of the enduring presence of Native Voices on the American landscape.

Publication of Native Voices is supported in part by a grant from The St. Paul Companies.

www.mnhs.org/mhspress

Manufactured in Canada.

10 9 8 7 6 5 4 3 2 1

International Standard Book Number 0-87351-400-9 (paper)

♾ The paper used in this publication meets the minimum requirements of the American National Standard for Information Sciences—Permanence for Printed Library Materials, ANSI Z39.48-1984.

The author wishes to thank Ted D. Mahto for permission to include his poem "Uncle Tomahawk" and passage from his novel *Cry in the Night*; and William J. Lawrence for permission to quote from his research paper "Legal Systems of the Red Lake Reservation."

The extracts on pages 1–4, 59-60, 62, and 70 are from *anishinabe adisokan* © 1970 by Gerald Vizenor; those on pages 7, 43, 51, 65, 109, and 134 are from *anishinabe nagamon* © 1965 by Gerald Robert Vizenor, © 1970 by Gerald Vizenor. The contents of pages 1–136 originally appeared as *The Everlasting Sky: New Voices of the People Named the Chippewa* © 1972 by Gerald Vizenor. The introduction on pages ix–xxvii and index on 137–140 are new to this edition © 2000 by Gerald Vizenor.

Library of Congress Cataloging-in-Publication Data

Vizenor, Gerald Robert, 1934–
The everlasting sky : voices of the Anishinabe people / Gerald Vizenor.
   p. cm. — (Native voices)
Originally published: New York : Crowell-Collier Press, 1972.
With new introd.
ISBN 0-87351-425-4 (pbk. : alk. paper)
1. Ojibwa Indians—Social conditions.
2. Ojibwa Indians—Government relations.
3. Ojibwa philosophy.
4. Indian reservations—Minnesota.
I. Title. II. Series

E99.C6 V59 2001
977.6'004973—dc21
                2001018705

For the old *anishinabe* woman
who cannot read this book
because she speaks only the language of the people

She lives on the White Earth Reservation
still naming the children
and staying beautiful
on scared herbs from the woodland

Contents

Introduction

George Morrison, the eminent painter and sculptor, re-sisted the notion that there were essential, traditional connections between culture and creative art. He argued that the identity of an artist, and in this sense the *anishinabe* artist, does not decide the meaning or determine the merit of the art. Native artists create more than the mere pictures of a culture. Morrison, an artist of international distinction, was born on the Grand Portage Reservation in Minnesota. He graduated from the Minneapolis School of Art, taught at the Rhode Island School of Design, and retired as a professor of art from the University of Minnesota.

I started the introduction to this new edition of *The Everlasting Sky* the very week that Morrison died at the

North Shore Hospital near the home and studio he had built on the shore of Lake Superior. At the time of his death he was at work on a series of paintings that create a sense of that imagic moment when the water on the horizon of the lake merges with the sky. He loved that northern landscape, and his abstract paintings announce the visionary power of a great *anishinabe* artist.

The Everlasting Sky was first published with no reference to my friend George Morrison. I was not pleased at the time because the original manuscript of the book had considered his significance as a creative artist; however, the editors at the Crowell-Collier Press in New York cut my chapter on "Anishinabe Artists." They reasoned that readers would rather look at the art than read about the artists. Moreover, the editors ruled against black and white reproductions of original art.

I wrote in the original manuscript of *The Everlasting Sky* that Morrison, who was in his late forties at the time:

> has had more than seventy public showings and exhibits of his work are in galleries in major cities in this country and in other parts of the world. The art critic for the *Minneapolis Star* wrote the following review of Morrison's paintings exhibited at the Kilbride-Bradley gallery in Minneapolis:
>
> "Morrison over the years has edged away from figurative painting and now is almost entirely devoted technically, to pattern and texture, in a rich repertoire of colors. . . his pieces project as visual music in various keys and harmonies.
>
> "The paintings seem to originate in a deep composure rather than stirred by external excitement, and they strike inner chords while pleasing the eye. They are animated by different schemes. In some there is a calm vertical flow, in

others there is a blazing centripetal movement. . . an art of
sensitivity and range, essentially lyrical and subjective. It
discloses an experienced skill in setting up the counterpoint
and tensions which induce you to gaze for a long time, seeking out the secrets imbedded there."

Morrison graduated from high school in Grand Marais,
Minnesota, near the Grand Portage Reservation.

I wrote in the first edition that he "has been on the
faculty of the Rhode Island School of Design and is now
a professor in the Indian Studies Department at the
University of Minnesota. He was awarded a Fulbright
scholarship to study art in Paris, France, and received
the John Hay Whitney fellowship to study the patterns
of *anishinabe* culture and art. He also attended the Art
Students League in New York for three years."

Morrison was dedicated to the freedom of creative expression, and, for that reason, would not burden an
artist with the political and cultural demands of identity.
He expressed "feelings about life" in his paintings,
"rather than what the society expects in traditional sym-
bols. He is not a traditionalist in the sense that he produces familiar images about cultural values."

Patrick Des Jarlait, another eminent *anishinabe* artist
featured in my original manuscript of *The Everlasting
Sky*, was more involved in the romantic images of the
traditional past than Morrison. "I give the picture of the
ideal people," he said at the kitchen table where he
painted after meals. "I try to bring out things in my
paintings that many white people may never see—the
happy people, like the happy mothers and fathers with
their children."

Des Jarlait was born on the Red Lake Reservation where he graduated from high school after attending a federal boarding school. He started drawing when he was four years old, he said, and has never stopped. "People like the muralistic quality of my paintings," he said. "My work is understood well by children because of the stories behind the paintings." Des Jarlait creates positive cultural pictures; the colors are warm, the artistic technique is delicate and concise, and the images are romantic. The original prints of his watercolor paintings, *The Wild Rice Harvest*, and *Red Lake Fisherman*, are very popular.

Morrison and Des Jarlait were creative artists, not ideologues, and yet their paintings could be used to show the diverse politics of *anishinabe* culture and identity. Regrettably, the essentialist notion that traditional culture marks the value of creative art has been used to exclude certain artists. Clearly, racialist representations and the politics of suitable traditions diminish the value of creative art.

Centuries ago the *anishinabe* were one of the most active and significant cultures on the continent. Then colonialism, disease, war, and removal to federal reservations weakened native communities everywhere in the country. In the past generation, however, the *anishinabe* have restored some of their original stature as a visionary culture by the creative work of painters, sculptors, and literary artists. By original styles, imagic scenes, and conceptual art, many contemporary *anishinabe* artists have reached beyond the bounds and obvious cues of tradition and culture.

David Bradley, for instance, is a painter who trans-
forms ordinary scenes and images by irony. Natives, in
his paintings, are always the active players in their own
history. One of his celebrated paintings, *How the West
Was Lost*, shows three men seated at a game of poker.
The cowboy has a card tucked in his belt. The Native
bets an ironic estate, a "Deed to Indian Land," with a
bird perched on his shoulder. The Mexican sits under a
crucifix. The three players are associated with the bottles
at their sides, Tequila, Fire Water, and Corn Whiskey.

Ted Mahto, the literary artist and philosopher, cele-
brates the natural *anishinabe* custom of daydreaming as
"a very constructive kind of behavior" in public schools.
And his ideas continue to enrich that cultural practice of
individual, visionary thought. "We are going to have to
find ways to recognize what it is that is happening to a
child when he daydreams, because this kind of visual
thinking, you know, might be of more value with respect
to learning how to live with one another than learning
how to work a mathematical problem," he told me in an
interview for the first edition of *The Everlasting Sky*.
There is "something spontaneous and religious about visual thinking which is being ignored in the public
schools."

Mahto was born on the Red Lake Reservation. He attended boarding schools, several colleges and universities, and for many years taught in the American Indian
Studies Department at the University of Minnesota. His
meditative ideas were as original then as they are now.
Many teachers have taken comfort in his thoughts and
used his insights to encourage their students.

Some public schools near reservations, however, have been very slow to appreciate *anishinabe* philosophies in their curricula. Professional certification, government regulations, and budget limitations are reasonable explanations for a deliberate academic manner, but too many *anishinabe* students have faced the daily burden of *manifest* manners, not academic manners; the apish continuance of manifest destiny.

The concept of manifest manners came to mind about the time this book was first published. I was then the director of a federal desegregation program at the Park Rapids High School in northern Minnesota. The service directive of the program was to reduce the high dropout rate among *anishinabe* students who were bused daily to the consolidated high school from the nearby White Earth Reservation. I conducted regular training sessions for teachers, bus drivers, and others, to change the conditions that caused so many bright *anishinabe* students to leave school before graduation. Most of these students had scored above the national average on standard tests in the elementary school on the reservation, but their scores declined after the first year in the high school. The conditions were situational not academic.

Mahto accepted my invitation to meet with teachers and *anishinabe* students to discuss his ideas about education. The students were amused by his stories and enriched by his regard for their significance as scholars and daydreamers, in the *anishinabe* tradition of visionaries. Some of the teachers were enticed by his respect for their profession, and noted his philosophical insights. The teachers were surely dedicated, generous, and sensitive, and yet many of them expressed the obvious racial notions of "cultural deprivation." They thought that *an-ishinabe* students were not as capable of abstract reasoning as other students. Some of these teachers were the unwitting agents of manifest manners.

Paulette Fairbanks said the transition from the reservation elementary school was one of the most difficult experiences in her life, and yet she graduated with honors from the same consolidated high school. "The transfer to college was easier for me than the transfer from Pine Point to Park Rapids," she said as a graduate student. Since then she has become a writer and national leader in education.

Jerome Buckanaga also graduated from the consolidated high school and a decade later he became the first *anishinabe* principal of the Pine Point School on the White Earth Reservation. Jerome was a pensive academic leader with a cool sense of humor and a clever use of political strategies. At the time of this story he had invited me to his home on a warm summer afternoon to discuss the high school program when a stranger knocked on the screen door.

Jerome stood at the screen as the man nervously introduced himself as the director of a new pioneer museum in Park Rapids. The director explained that he wanted Buckanaga, an *anishinabe* educator, to sanction the display of a human skeleton in the museum. Jerome stared at the man for a strategic moment and then asked him if that was the same skeleton that had been stored in the closet. Yes, it was in the closet, said the director who was too nervous to appreciate the irony. Sure, you can hang that skeleton out, said Buckanaga.

The director expressed his gratitude, and confessed

that he was worried about being denied permission to show the skeleton. Jerome listened and then asked the stranger if he wanted to know why he had agreed. Yes, of course, said the director. Buckanaga said, That's a white skeleton, so you can do anything you want with it. The director was distracted, disconcerted, and even bedeviled by the sudden racialist turn of skeletal events.

Jerome told me later than he had no idea if the skeleton was white, but he took a chance that the director would never hang a white skeleton in a pioneer museum. By this strategy he may have saved an *anishinabe* skeleton from public display.

The *anishinabe* past was once described as an absence, either by historical summaries of cultural dominance, by the nostalgia over lost traditions, or by the sentiments of tragedy. Clearly, the strategies and philosophies articulated by this generation of *anishinabe* storiers have contributed to a sense of presence not absence. Since this book was first published thousands of *anishinabe* scholars have graduated from colleges and universities; thousands more have pursued professional degrees in medicine, law, social work, and education. Many more have selected careers in law enforcement, real estate, journalism, banking, business, public relations, and politics.

Hennepin County District Judge Robert Blaeser, for instance, who was born on the White Earth Reservation, served as the chief judge of the Juvenile Court. He was the first *anishinabe* judge in the county, and the third in the state. Kimberly Blaeser, his sister, is a poet, literary scholar, and professor at the University of Wisconsin, Milwaukee.

I could only have imagined at the time *The Everlasting Sky* was first published that casinos would transform many reservation communities. The incredible wealth from this dubious industry has provided medical and dental care, endowed educational programs, new housing, and other necessary services to many *anishinabe* communities. Readily, elected reservation leaders have become more active in state and national politics. And, at the same time, so much easy wealth has invited corruption. I doubt that many readers of the first edition of this book would have accepted a prediction that several reservations in the state might be converted not by enlightened federal policies but by the economic riches of casinos.

Norman Crooks, the former chairman of the Shakopee Mdewakanton Sioux Community at Prior Lake, established the Little Six Bingo Palace in 1982, one of the first bingo operations with large jackpots in Minnesota. Mystic Lake, the subsequent name of the casino, a monument to simulated traditions, has become one of the largest in the country.

The Fond du Lac Reservation tribal council, and the mayor of the city of Duluth, proposed a venture casino as a source of revenue for the city and the reservation community. Some fifteen years ago this preposterous operation opened in a converted Sears building in downtown Duluth. The Fond du Luth Gaming Commission, as it was aptly named, reported at the time that "never before in history had off-reservation land been taken into trust as Indian land for the purpose of gaming." William Houle, then the elected chairman of the tribal council, pointed out that the casino was supported by both state and federal politicians. "Gaming has always been part of our culture, and now it is an integral part of our economy as well," said Houle. As the number of casinos have increased in the past decade, so too have the critics.

The Native American Indian gaming industry has grown from a few hundred million to an estimated ten billion dollars a year in the past decade. The critical debates are over accountability and who decides if the money is to be invested or paid to designated tribal members. Forty-eight "tribes have obtained approval from the Bureau of Indian Affairs to transfer casino profits directly to members," reported the New York Times. Payments, for instance, "range up to $900,000 a year for each of the more than 200 members of the Shakopee Mdewakanton Dakota Sioux Community in Minnesota." I wrote in *Manifest Manners: Narratives on Postindian Survivance* that the revenue from reservation casinos has not created a state of real political power; rather, the wealth has incited envies and the enemies of tribal sovereignty. Yet, in spite of the great risks of envy, who can argue against the fast money that has reduced poverty and increased employment on reservations?

William Lawrence, a law school graduate who once ran for the position of tribal chairman on the Red Lake Reservation, has carried on a great tradition of reservation newspapers. The editor and publisher of *The Progress*, the first *anishinabe* newspaper published on the White Earth Reservation, announced in the first issue, March 25, 1886, that the "novelty of a newspaper published upon this reservation may cause many to be wary in their support, and this from a fear that it may be revolutionary in character." *The Progress* was indeed revolutionary, and so too is the *Native American Press/Ojibwe News*, a controversial weekly newspaper founded in 1988 by Lawrence. He writes editorials on a wide range of economic and political issues on reservations, but, a century later, with a more conservative nature than the editors of *The Progress*. Lawrence has been especially critical of those accountable for casino money.

Melanie Benjamin "has a clear mandate from the Mille Lacs people to bring open and accountable government to the Mille Lacs Reservation," he wrote in an editorial after Benjamin defeated the incumbent Marge Anderson in the election for chief executive of the Mille Lacs Band of Ojibwe. "That means that she must undertake and accomplish two major tasks as soon as possible. The first being to find out where all the casino money is going and has gone for the past eight years. And second is to find out what the Mille Lacs Band of Ojibwe Corporation Commission is doing." The Commission has made investment decisions.

Casino money, obscure investments, and vested interests on reservations have been featured in newspaper stories more often than individual entrepreneurs, but private enterprises have always been a significant part of the *anishinabe* economic history. Casinos are corporate, political ventures while entrepreneurs and privately owned commerce creates an active economic system in reservation communities. Surely, from active fur trade routes across the continent, to moose burgers, and spirit catchers, the anishinabe are evermore portrayed as independent, enterprising, and visionary. Louise Erdrich, for instance, the author of *Love Medicine* and other novels, and Dennis Banks, the radical activist and elder petitioner, have only recently become entrepreneurs. Erdrich established Birchbark Books, Herbs, and Native Arts, an independent bookstore in Minneapolis. Banks returned to the Leech Lake Reservation and formed the Dennis Banks Wild Rice and Natural Organic Foods Company. Japanese investors have expressed an interest in his line of products, in part, because he published his autobiography in Japan. The book has not yet been translated into English. Native American entrepreneurs with name and cultural recognition may have a better chance of success in very competitive local and global markets.

Casino riches and the politics of envy have changed many reservations in the past decade, but in my view the most significant and lasting favors in *anishinabe* communities have been made by creative artists. The many *anishinabe* painters, poets, novelists, and other artists have by their shows, exhibitions, readings, and publications continued the sovereignty of a visionary culture.

The Everlasting Sky was never a cultural measure of service to *anishinabe* communities, but those mentioned in the first edition of the book have continued their good work in education and public service. Bonnie Wallace, for instance, who was born on the Fond du Lac Reservation, graduated from the University of Minnesota. For many years she directed education programs at Augsburg College in Minneapolis, and then returned to the reservation to continue her service in education.

George Mitchell, an activist who was born on the White Earth Reservation, continues his criticism of government services. He was the first *anishinabe* candidate, a generation ago, to run for alderman in Minneapolis. "I will admit that I am a bitter man," he said in a campaign speech at the time. "Bitter because while driving here tonight I see the same things I saw ten years ago. Muddy roads that remind me of things similar or worse than those on the reservation, condemned houses, well-lighted liquor stores and poorly lighted streets.

"Who knows more about these conditions than the people who live here? We have heard for a long time how government is for the people, but how can a government without the people be for the people?" Mitchell lost the election, but his urgent thoughts have never been forgotten. His ideas have become part of a collective memory of change in *anishinabe* communities.

Clyde Bellecourt continues to be one of the most controversial *anishinabe* militants in the American Indian Movement. He has served more than fifteen years in correctional institutions for various crimes. "They told me I already had two strikes against me," he told me in an interview for the first edition of *The Everlasting Sky*. "First I was an *indian,* and second I was a convicted felon."

Bellecourt has posed as a victim of the criminal justice system for more than thirty years. Since the first edition of this book he has not earned unequivocal praise from *anishinabe* communities; not because of his uncertain protests of rivals, conspirators, and federal agencies, or even his morose, abusive manner, but because of his criminal activities.

Bellecourt "has told his story so many times, a story that takes him from the White Earth Indian Reservation to Wounded Knee to federal prison," and back to Franklin Avenue in Minneapolis, reported Kim Ode in the *Minneapolis Star Tribune*. "It unfolds as easily as a school teacher's lesson, earnest yet having acquired a rehearsed quality over the years. Someday, his account of his more recent life as a cocaine addict may take on the same rote nature. For now, though, he speaks. . . .with more spontaneity, blurting details of mirrors and razor blades, then proceeding haltingly, as if sifting the right words from kilos of possibilities. He was convicted in April 1986 of selling LSD to undercover agents." Bellecourt "pleaded guilty inside the courtroom and claimed entrapment outside it. He served twenty-two months of a five-year federal prison term and emerged determined to improve the life of Indian children.

"Bellecourt may have changed, but not everyone is buying it," observed Ode. "Those who dislike him refuse to speak on the record, saying that they fear reprisals. Word of a newspaper article ignites the grapevine and the telephone rings with anonymous voices, all of whom identify themselves as American Indians, urging caution."

Bellecourt had been under surveillance for several months by agents of the Drug Enforcement Administration. He was indicted by a federal grand jury on nine felony counts. He pleaded guilt to one count of drug distribution as part of a negotiated plea bargain with federal attorneys. Bellecourt was guilty of distributing dangerous drugs but he did not go directly to prison.

Federal District Judge Paul Magnuson munificently allowed Bellecourt to attend a scheduled sun dance ceremony in Arizona before he surrendered to federal authorities to begin his five year sentence.

The Chippewa, Ojibway, and Ojibwe are the same culture as the *anishinabe,* or anishinabeg, the plural in the language. The family was the basic political and economic unit in the woodland and one of the primary sources of personal identity. The individual was known to others by nicknames. The *oshki anishinabe* are the new people of the woodland.

"Before you begin listening to the *oshki anishinabe* speaking in this book, please write a short definition of the word *indian,*" I wrote in the introduction to the first edition of *The Everlasting Sky.* The word *indian*, always printed in lower case italics to draw attention to the simulation of hundreds of cultures in one name, reveals the burden of occidental, colonial dominance. "Then as you read and listen to the *oshki anishinabe*, the new people of the woodland who bear cultural simulations and invented names, express their anger and dreams and fears, remember what you think the word *indian* means." Native names and *anishinabe* words are italicized for emphasis in the narrative. The phonetic spelling of *anishinabe* words conforms to the entries transcribed in *A Dictionary of the Otchipwe Language* by Bishop Baraga. The transcription of certain words, such as anishinaabe, varies in *A Concise Dictionary of Minnesota Ojibwe,* edited by John Nichols and Earl Nyholm, which was published after the first edition of *The Everlasting Sky.*

Nichols wrote in *Ojibwewi-Ikidowinan: An Ojibwe Word Resource Book* that the "Ojibwe language is one language of a wide-spread family of North American Indian languages known as Algonquian language family, one of many such families of languages. Ojibwe is spoken by perhaps forty-thousand to fifty-thousand people in the north-central part of the continent. Although the English name 'Chippewa' is commonly used both for the people and their ancestral language in Michigan, Minnesota, North Dakota, and Wisconsin, in the language itself the people are the *Anishinaabeg* and the language is called *Anishinaabemowin*."

"The Four Ages of Man" was first printed more than a century ago in *The Progress*, a weekly newspaper published on the White Earth Reservation. The story has been edited to include *manabozho*, or *naanabozho*, the woodland trickster, and other *anishinabe* words. Minnesota has seven *anishinabe* reservations: Bois Forte, or Nett Lake, Fond du Lac, Grand Portage, Leech Lake, Mille Lacs, White Earth, and Red Lake. The *anishinabe* signed ten treaties with the federal government in the nineteenth century. These treaties and other agreements and executive orders ceded resources, sections of land, and established reservations. The first treaty at Fond du Lac, in 1826, for instance, ceded "the right to search for and carry away any metals or minerals." The last treaty between the *anishinabe* and the federal government was signed in 1867.

"Treaties with the Ojibway living in the region that became Minnesota were first signed in 1825, in an effort to secure peace between them and the Dakota," wrote

Elizabeth Ebbott in *Indians in Minnesota*, a crucial survey edited by Judith Rosenblatt. "A line was drawn diag-
onally across the state, with each group to remain in its
own area. In 1837 a large area, including portions of
Michigan, Wisconsin, and Minnesota north of the 1825
line extending to the Crow Wing River, was ceded by the
Mississippi band. The Indians were not required to
move." Later treaties removed the *anishinabe* to reservations.

The Minnesota Chippewa Tribe is a corporate federation of six *anishinabe* reservations. The Tribal Executive
Committee of the federation is formed by two elected
members from each of the six reservations. The Red
Lake Reservation, located on original land that was
never ceded in treaties, has an independent constitutional government and is not a member of the federation.

Bois Forte, or the Nett Lake Reservation, is located in
the northern counties of Saint Louis and Koochiching.
The government center is in the community of Nett
Lake. "The reservation has beautiful pine forests, large
lakes, and many streams. It is noted for its fine wild
rice," observed Elizabeth Ebbott in *Indians in
Minnesota*. About forty percent of the original treaty
land established by the federal government in 1866 is
now owned by *anishinabe* members of the reservation.

The Fond du Lac Reservation is located in Saint
Louis and Carlton counties, about twenty miles west of
Duluth. Close to eighty percent of the original treaty
land established by treaty in 1854 is owned by the members of the reservation.

The Grand Portage Reservation is located in the

northeastern corner of the state on the Pigeon River, about thirty miles north of Grand Marais in Cook County. The reservation was created in 1854 by the La Pointe Treaty. The Northwest Company established "grand northern depot," a late eighteenth century fur trade post at "Grand Portage, near the mouth of Pigeon River," wrote William Warren, the first published *anishinabe* historian, in *History of the Ojibway Nation*.

The Leech Lake Reservation is located in five counties in north central Minnesota. The Mississippi River runs through Cass Lake and Winnibigoshish Lake on the reservation. The first reservation was created by federal treaty in 1855, and then the consolidated reservation was established in 1864. Several years later the area of the reservation was changed by treaty and executive orders. About twenty percent of the original treaty land is owned by *anishinabe* members of the reservation. The *anishinabe* live in Onigum, Federal Dam, Cass Lake, Bena, Ball Club, Deer River, and other communities.

The Mille Lacs Reservation is located in four counties in central Minnesota. The reservation was established by treaty in 1855. "Later treaties and acts of Congress were intended to make the Indians move," wrote Elizabeth Ebbot in *Indians in Minnesota*.

The White Earth Reservation is located in Becker, Clearwater, and Mahnomen counties in northwestern Minnesota. Nearby is the source of the Mississippi River in Lake Itaska. The reservation was established by treaty in 1867. Only about eight percent of the original treaty land is now owned by *anishinabe* members of the reservation. The Red Lake Reservation is located in nine counties in northwestern Minnesota. The main reservation was never ceded to the federal government, although certain areas, such as land at Northwest Angle, were ceded and later restored to the reservation. The Red Lake *anishinabe* were never removed *to* a reservation; rather, they continue to live on "diminished" but original tribal land, and maintain a separate government outside of state jurisdiction. The reservation is governed by an elected council, and the hereditary leaders continue to serve as advisors. The reservation maintains an independent police and court system, and the public school on the reservation is an independent district.

Gerald Vizenor

The Four Ages
of Man

"My grandson, the land which you intended to visit is infested with many evil spirits and the followers of those who eat human flesh. . . . No one who has ever been within their power has ever been known to return.

"First they charm their victims by the sweetness of their songs, then they strangle and devour them, but your principal enemy will be the *great gambler* who has never been beaten and who lives beyond the realm of darkness . . . therefore, my grandson, I would beseech you not to undertake so dangerous a journey."

And *manabozho* listened to his grandmother. But the folk hero of the *anishinabe* felt that he was brave and should know no fear. The warning words of *nokomiss*, his grandmother, were unheeded.

Manabozho consulted with the different birds and animals and good spirits and it was decided that the owl would lend him his eyes and the firefly would accompany him to light the way through the realms of darkness. . . .

The path which *manabozho* was traveling led him through swamps and over high mountains and by yawning chasms where he saw the hideous stare of a thousand gleaming eyes . . . and he heard the groans and hisses and yells of countless fiends gloating over their many victims of sin and shame . . . and he knew that this was the place where the *great gambler* consigned the spirits of his many victims. . . .

Approaching the entrance of the wigwam, *manabozho* raised the mat of scalps which served as the door and found himself in the presence of the *great gambler*. He was a curious-looking being who seemed almost round in shape. . . .

"So *manabozho*, you, too, have come to try your luck, and you think I am not a very expert gambler," the *great gambler* said, reaching for his war club and chuckling a horrible sound of scorn and ridicule.

"All of these hands you see hanging around this wigwam are the hands of your people who came here to gamble. They thought as you are now thinking. They played and lost their lives.

"I seek no one to come and gamble with me but those who would gamble their lives. . . . Remember that I demand the lives of those who gamble with me and lose. . . . I keep the scalps and ears and hands and the rest of the body is given to my friends the flesh eaters. . . . The spirits of those who have lost their lives I consign to the land of darkness,'' the *great gambler* said, still grinning with confidence. "Now I have spoken and we will play.''

The *great gambler* took in his hands the *anishinabe* dish game and said to *manabozho*: "Here are the four figures, the four ages of man, which I will shake in the dish four times, and if they assume a standing position each time, then I am the winner . . . should they fall, then you are the winner.''

Laughing, *manabozho* looked at the dish and the four ages of man and told the *great gambler* beyond the realm of darkness, "Very well, we will play. But it is customary for the party who is challenged to play any game to have the last play.''

The *great gambler* consented while taking up the dish for the first time and striking it on the ground. The four figures were all in a standing position. This was repeated twice more by the *great gambler* and each time the four figures representing the four ages of man fell in a standing position.

The destiny of *manabozho* and the *anishinabe* people depended upon the one chance remaining. Should the four ages of man fall in the standing position *manabozho* would lose and the spirit of the *anishinabe* people would be consigned to the flesh eaters in the land of darkness.

When the *great gambler* prepared to make the final shake of the game *manabozho* drew near and when the dish came down to the ground he made a teasing whistle on the wind and all four figures of the four ages of man fell.

The *anishinabe* people had not lost their spirit to the land of darkness. When *manabozho* seized the dish from the *great gambler* he said, "Now it is my turn, and should I win, you will lose your life. . . ."

1

The Sacred Names
Were Changed

The traditions handed down from father to son were
held very sacred . . . half of these are not known by
the white people, however far their researches may
have extended. . . .

—George Copway, *anishinabe* missionary, 1847

In the original tales of the people the sacred *migis* shell
of the *anishinabe* spirit—a shell resembling the cow-
rie, which is still used to decorate ceremonial vest-
ments—arose from the eastern sea and moved along
the inland waters guiding the people through the
sleeping sun of the woodland to *bawitig*—the long
rapids in the river.

The *anishinabe*—the original people of the woodland—believe they were given wisdom and life color
from the reflection of the sun on the sacred shell
during this long migration. Five hundred years ago the
migis shell appeared in the sun for the last time at
moningwanekaning in *anishinabe kitchigame*—La

Pointe on Madeline Island in Lake Superior—the great sea of the *anishinabe*.

The people measured life in the circles of the sun and moon and human heart. Trailing the summer shores of *kitchigame* to the hardwoods and maple sugar swamps and stands of *manomin*—wild rice— many families of the *anishinabe* returned each winter to *moningwanekaning* and told stories of the summer past.

In the seventeenth century the first voyageurs and missionaries of the Old World established a fur-trading post on the island near the sacred community of the people. While showing the New World *discoverers* how to endure the long woodland winters, less than half of the *anishinabe* survived the first pestilence of the white man—a severe smallpox epidemic.

More than a century ago the *anishinabe* historian and legislator William Warren described in his *History of the Ojibways* a copper plate with incised marks showing three *anishinabe* generations living on the island before the voyageurs arrived. Warren wrote that he had viewed the copper historical record of the people in the middle of the nineteenth century, by which time it had eight incised marks. Warren estimated each generation to be forty years.

The expanding interests of the predatory fur trade in the woodland—spurred by the Old World bourgeois demand for felt hats—drew the *anishinabe* to other fur-trading posts among the *dakota* and other tribal families with beaver peltry and other hides in exchange for firearms and diluted intoxicants. The *anishinabe* came in conflict with the *dakota* and other tribal families of the woodland.

With rifles the *anishinabe* easily defeated the woodland *dakota* and drove them from the rich wild-rice lands in northern Minnesota. The *anishinabe* sang this song about the wounded *dakota* men—a song of woodland peace:

> moving forward and back
> from the woodland to the prairie
> dakota women
> weeping
> as they gather
> their wounded men
> the sound of their weeping
> comes back to us

The fur trade interposed an economic anomaly between the intuitive rhythm of woodland life and the equipoise of the *anishinabe* spirit. While the people were reluming the human unity of tribal life, thousands of white settlers took their land under new laws and enslaved the *anishinabe* in the fury of discovery.

The rhythm of the woodland was broken by the marching cadence of Christian patriotism. The *anishinabe* orators of the *mang odem*, the loon family, the legions of the *makwa odem*, the bear family, and the people of the *amik odem*, the beaver family, were colonized and mythologized and alienated from their woodland life and religion while the voices of the conquering crusaders in the New World rang with freedom. The woodland identity of the people was homogenized in patent histories, and the religious songs of the *anishinabe* were Latinized by nervy missionaries.

The *anishinabe* lost their land and were renamed. In nine treaties with the federal government the people were given the invented names *chippewa* and *ojibway*.

More than a century ago Henry Rowe Schoolcraft, a student of geology and mineralogy, named the *anishinabe*—the original people of the woodland—the *ojibwa*. The meaning of the invented name is not clear in the *anishinabe* language, but Schoolcraft reasoned that the root meaning of the word *ojibwa* described the peculiar nasal sound of the *anishinabe* voice.

George Copway, the *anishinabe* missionary among his own people, explained that the *anishinabe* were called the *ojibway* because of the moccasins they wore, which were "gathered on the top from the tip of the toe, and at the ankle."

In his book *The Traditional History and Characteristic Sketches of the Ojibway Nation,* published in London in 1850, Copway wrote that ". . . no other *indians* wore this style of footgear, and it was on account of this peculiarity that they were called *ojibway*, the signification of which is *gathering.*"

William Warren takes exception to both definitions of the word *ojibway*. In his *History of the Ojibway Nation,* Warren, who was the first person of *anishinabe* ancestry to serve in the Minnesota State Legislature, wrote the following about the invented names:

"The word is composed of *ojib*—pucker up—and *abew*—to roast—and it means *to roast till puckered up. . . .*

"It is well authenticated by their traditions, and by the writings of *their early white discoverers*, that before they became acquainted with, and made use of the firearm and other European weapons of war, instead of their primitive bow and arrow and war-club, their wars with other tribes were less deadly, and they were more accustomed to secure captives, whom under the uncontrolled feeling incited by aggravated wrong, and revenge for similar injuries, they tortured by fire in various ways.

"The name of *abwenag*—roasters—which the *ojibways* have given to the *dakota* . . . originated in their roasting their captives, and it is as likely that the word *ojibwa*—to roast till puckered up—originated in the same manner. . . .

"The name of the tribe has been most commonly spelt, *chippeway*, and is thus laid down in *our* different treaties with *them*, and officially used by *our* Government."

Warren was born on Madeline Island in Lake Superior before reservations were established. He may have been rejecting his *anishinabe* identity by emphasizing the fantasies of savagery and cannibalism common in the minds of many white people a century ago. He had left the woodland family of his birth, and like many *oshki anishinabe* of today, he succeeded in the dominant society. His success changed the view of his own past and the past of the *anishinabe*.

In a different chapter of his book, Warren explains without derogatory cultural fantasies that the invented name of the tribe "does not date far back. As a race or distinct people *they* denominate themselves *anishin-abe.*''

Schoolcraft, who married an *anishinabe* woman and became an official *indian* agent for the government, not only invented the name *ojibwa,* but he categorized the many families of the people living in the woodland as the *algic* tribes. He invented the word *algic* from the word *algonquin,* which was a name invented earlier by the French to identify a different woodland tribe *they* had discovered. The word *algonquin* is still used to describe several tribes of the people who speak a similar language.

The story is told that the word *ojibwa* invented by Schoolcraft was misunderstood by a traveling federal bureaucrat who heard *chippewa* for *ojibwa.* Once recorded in the treaties between the *anishinabe* and the federal government, the invented name was a matter of law.

The *anishinabe* must still wear the invented names. The tragedy is that today many young *oshki anishin-abe* do not know the difference between the names. Some believe they are the *chippewa,* or the *ojibway.*

Almost a century ago Bishop Baraga published the first dictionary of the *anishinabe* language. Baraga, while living on Madeline Island, interpreted *anishina-bemowin*—the language of the *anishinabe*—according to Old World Latin linguistic structures. The diction-ary is one of the few records to understand the words of the past. The *anishinabe* did not have a written language. The *anishinabe* past was a visual memory and oratorical gesture of dreams and songs and tales incised as pictomyths on birch bark scrolls.

The following *anishinabe* words with definitions are quoted from Baraga's *Dictionary of the Otchipwe Language* to show the confusion caused by the invented names for the people:

> *nind*—the personal pronoun in *anishinabemowin*
> *nind ojibiwa*—I write or mark on some object
> *ojibiigan*—writing, writ, document
> *odishkwagami*—*algonquin indian*
> *otchipwe*—*chippewa indian*
> *otchipwemowin*—the *chippewa* language
> *anishinabe*—human being, man, woman or child
> *anishinabemowin*—the *indian* language
> *anishinabe ijitwawin*—*indian* pagan religion
> *nind anishinabem*—I speak *indian*
> *nind anishinabew*—I am a human being, also, I am
>   an *indian*

Baraga defines *otchipwemowin* as the *chippewa* language and *anishinabemowin* as the *indian* language and he defines *indian* as *anishinabe.* There is of course no such language as the *indian* language because the word *indian* was also invented, homogenizing more than three hundred distinct tribal cultures.

Today the people named the *odjibwa, otchipwe, ojibway, chippewa, chippeway* and *indian* still speak of themselves in the language of their religion as the *anishinabe.*

Not only have many tribal names been invented, but the personal descriptive names of the people have been changed and translated without meaning. In the past an *anishinabe* child was given a sacred name by a close member of the family. The sacred name was not the last name of the family but a unique spiritual name known from a dream or vision. The descriptive names translated by missionaries and government officials were translations of nicknames. The actual *anishinabe* sacred names were not revealed to strangers and were seldom translated.

Only two generations ago the *anishinabe* were systematically forbidden to speak their language and practice their religion. White people in the dominant society thought that tribal people were pagan primitives who must be changed. *Anishinabe* children were removed from their families and placed in federal boarding schools where they were physically punished for speaking the language of their heart—the language of their woodland identity.

Today few young people speak the *anishinabe* language. The culture of the *anishinabe* past has been homogenized by the dominant society for use in patent educational curriculum units. In classrooms today *oshki anishinabe* children are summoned to be proud of their invented *indian* and *chippewa* heritage. When a young *oshki anishinabe* is expected to know several thousand years of his history only in the superior language and superior cultural values of the dominant society his identity is a dangerous burden.

The cultural and political histories of the *anishinabe* were written in the language of those who invented the *indian*, renamed the tribes, allotted the land, divided ancestry by geometric degrees—the federal government identifies the *anishinabe* by degrees of *indian* blood—and categorized identity by the geography of colonial reservations. The inventions of the dominant society have nothing to do with the heart of the people.

2

Something the White Man Named

The name does not date far back. As a race or distinct people *they* denominate themselves *anishinabe. . . .*

—William Warren, *anishinabe* historian and legislator, 1852

Dressed in buckskin vest and beaded necklace, Harold Goodsky, the *oshki anishinabe* probation officer, leaned back in his swivel chair with his feet crossed on top of his desk. It was the end of the week and he was thinking about driving north to his home on the Nett Lake Reservation.

He picked up his pen and tapped on a pad of paper. The city was hot and oppressive and he wanted to tell stories in the *anishinabe* language and laugh with his family and friends on the reservation.

He tapped his pen, denting the paper, and thought about driving home alone to be there in the morning when the sun came up.

14

The sound of honking horns from the cars crowded in rush-hour traffic on the streets outside reached his office in the courthouse. On the reservation the air would be clean and he could think about himself again. He pitched forward in his chair, dropping his feet to the floor, and started writing *indian, indian, indian* . . .

"I sat at my desk one day and wrote the word *indian*," Goodsky said later. "I wrote it over and over again . . . *indian, indian, indian* . . . and I asked myself—why, how, what does it mean . . .

"I just sat there writing *indian, indian, indian,* over and over again. I was really befuddled. . . . I don't know what I was thinking about all the time," he said, sitting on the front steps of his apartment at dusk a week after he returned to the city from the reservation.

"Who am I?" he asked himself, "—something the white man named and made up. . . . I was chained in a dream and thought about us all being named by a psychopath like Columbus. . . .

"But I couldn't be me without my color," he said, holding his hands up and turning them over and over. "I would be nobody without my color. . . . I don't know about the name *indian*, I don't know that much about history, but I know I have my color."

Goodsky has his color and speaks the *anishinabe* language, but being an *indian* is a very complex experience. The dominant society has created a homogenized history of tribal people for a television culture. Being an *indian* is a heavy burden to the *oshki anishinabe* because white people know more about the *indian* they invented than anyone. The experts and cultural hobbyists never miss a chance to authenticate the scraps of romantic history dropped by white travelers through the *indian country* centuries ago. White people are forever projecting their dreams of a perfect life through the invention of the *indian*—and then they expect an *oshki anishinabe* to not only fulfill the invention but to authenticate third-hand information about the tribal past. The dominant society expects the *oshki anishinabe* to know about the histories written by white people, while few white people are familiar with the material written by the *anishinabe*. What the *anishinabe* has told of the past seldom slips through the pale template of homogenized history.

For example, the organization identified as *Indian Guides* is a group of fathers and sons who take *indian* names like *laughing water*, and *running deer*, and *little bear* and *big bear*, and wear imitation feathers and headbands and felt vests with monogrammed tribal names. All this imitating is for the stated purpose of bringing father and son closer together.

The group responded to criticism from several *oshki anishinabe* leaders by inviting the *indians* to join *Indian Guides*, thus proving they were not discriminating against a minority group.

The names of many rivers, towns, mountains, hills, lakes, animals, foods and private companies are words borrowed from the invented *indian* language and from the *anishinabe* language. Everywhere the *oshki anishinabe* are aware of the invented names—chippewa falls . . . indian chief inhaler . . . chippewa springs . . . indian summer—and are summoned by white people to be proud that so many *indian* things are being shared by everyone. The *oshki anishinabe* ask that the dominant society share the burdens of poverty and high infant mortality and a shorter life expectancy— when will white people stop playing *indian* long enough to share the responsibilities of *real* people?

White students at a small college in the southern part of the State of Minnesota were asked to define the word *indian* before two *oshki anishinabe* speakers were to discuss the programs of the people. The following are typical definitions offered by the students:

> Indian is a cultural nationality.
> They are a race with a distinct culture.
> Real Americans.
> Redskins.
> A member of the mongolian race.
> Indian means friend.
> A human being.
> Indian is a person.
> Indian is an ethnic group.
> A wild savage.
> Indian means man.

The white students in the audience admitted that they often use the word *indian* in speaking or writing but the word meant something different to each person. Only two students of about five hundred who responded defined an *indian* as a native of India. Two students were aware that, through a navigational error, more than three hundred distinct tribal cultures on this continent were homogenized by mistake as the *indians*. Many of those white students who were in the audience that day are now teaching school. Some of them may have *oshki anishinabe* children in their classrooms.

The *oshki anishinabe* high school students attending the Youth Leadership Training Program at Bemidji State College several years ago were asked to write anonymously about what it means to be an *indian*. Four students from four different reservations in the state wrote the following:

STUDENT FROM THE NETT LAKE RESERVATION
I think the *chippewa indian* is slowly dying. Right now there are plenty of *indians* in the United States but very few full-blooded *ojibways*. In Minnesota there is a large number of *indians* but also the fact that they're of mixed blood. Right now the modern *indian* has very many opportunities, the same as a white man. There are some that work their way up to a high position at their place of income and in the community. Yet there are others who don't seem to care. . . .

STUDENT FROM THE LEECH LAKE RESERVATION
I think the *indians* are great lovers. . . . A lot of *indians* have a little French blood in them. The French are supposed to be great lovers. . . . Maybe that is why they are great lovers. And they don't like to be seen making love because they are not as proud as they used to be. . . .

STUDENT FROM THE FOND DU LAC RESERVATION
I think there is a little difference between the *indians* and other people. The *indians* have a little darker skin and

some are smarter than the rest. Some people judge the *indians* by their outward appearance. They don't know what's going on inside. The *indians* also are very shy, and some talk right out when they are spoken to. Some have a very bad temper, when they are joked around with they get mad and blow up. With others they take it as a joke as it was meant to be. The *indian* girls are the love type whenever they see a cute boy. They giggle or try to make a hit. One thing about being an *indian*, you have to take things as they come, like when other people talk about you, you just don't blame them because they don't know what they're talking about. . . .

STUDENT FROM THE WHITE EARTH RESERVATION

Almost all of my heritage is European, about one fourth is *indian*. Of my four nationalities, French, English, Irish and *indian*, I am most proud of my *indian* heritage. There are a lot of *indians* I know who are ashamed of their *indian* heritage, but if you really stop and think about it, why should they? They probably feel that their ancestors were very barbaric but they were very artistic people. . . .

The *oshki anishinabe* are many colors and many different religions, and they have black eyes and blue eyes, blond hair and straight black hair, and they live on and off the reservation, in small towns, remote communities and in the city. The new people of the woodland have intermarried with the French—for more than two hundred years—and with the Finnish, German, Swedish, English, Irish and Norwegian people who have settled in the state. In *oshki anishinabe* humor those people with Finnish blood are identified as the *findian tribe*. Whatever the color of the skin and the politics, the *oshki anishinabe* come together with complex cultural diversity and speak of themselves as being of one tribe.

In politics the *oshki anishinabe* are conservative and liberal, radical and moderate, and a few people hang in the middle and are identified as the *hang-around-the-fort indians*.

A small number of *oshki anishinabe* dismiss the tribal past as a pagan and idolatrous life and identify as a special *indian Christian* in the organization of the *American Indian Evangelical Church.*

On the cover of a weekly church program is the picture of Iver Grover, *oshki anishinabe* minister of the *indian church,* smiling in headdress and buckskin shirt with an open Bible in his hand.

The Reverend Mr. Grover in a testimonial tells the few people attending his church each Sunday morning that he "took part in all the religious ceremonies of my *indian* people—the feast offerings of wild rice and berries . . . I had a sack full of idolatrous objects which I reverenced—skins of animals and birds and carved wooden images. For all those years I followed this form of false worship faithfully. . . .

"Since my conversion, God has called me to witness for Him and to win souls for Christ among my own people—the *indian* American. I preach in *chippewa* and English. . . ."

Most *oshki anishinabe* identify as Christians and belong in large numbers to the Episcopalian and Catholic churches, and some in fewer numbers attend other Protestant churches in the city and on the reservation. Very few *oshki anishinabe* speak the *anishinabe* language or practice herbal medicine, and few understand the *midewiwin*—the original spiritual life of the people—but most *oshki anishinabe* would like to know about herbal medicine and the religion of the tribal past.

Every year there are more and more special programs for young *oshki anishinabe* to learn the songs and dream language of the past. For example, the Minnesota State Department of Education offered a summer *anishinabe* language camp where *oshki anishinabe* children were taught language, culture, arts and crafts, singing, drumming and dancing by the elders of the tribe. The spiritual links with the past were resumed.

The *kiowa* novelist and teacher N. Scott Momaday, who won the Pulitzer Prize for his novel *House Made of Dawn*, told a group of *oshki anishinabe* and other tribal people at a conference on education that "the *indian* has been for a long time generalized in the imagination of the white man. Denied the acknowledgment of individuality and change, he has been made to become in theory what he could not become in fact, a synthesis of himself. . . .

"Now this is what I mean: the Navajo is an American *indian* but the American *indian* is not conversely a Navajo. He is rather to the public mind that lowly specter that stood for two hundred years in the way of civilization—who was removed time and again by force and who was given in defeat that compensation which we call *savage nobility*. . . .

"The relationship between the white man and the red was in a sense doomed from the onset by a conflict of attitudes and the disposition of intolerance . . . the persistent attempt to generalize the *indian* has resulted in a delusion and a nomenclature of half-truths. . . ."

A young *oshki anishinabe* college student climbs off his motorcycle in front of the Minneapolis Institute of Arts. He has long black hair and is dressed in a beaded buckskin vest and an imitation bear-claw necklace. He is tall and husky and smiles most of his waking hours. Born at Ponemah on the Red Lake Reservation, he was three years old when his family moved to the city. He graduated from a public school in the city. He has dark eyes and dark skin and knows nothing about *anishinabe* religion and does not speak the language of the tribal past. Stretched out on a couch with his legs crossed over the arm, and smiling, he answers the following questions:

Do you believe in anishinabe *medicine?*
Never heard of it. I was raised among the whites . . . and I'm not the only one who was.

What is your religion?
You could call me sort of an atheist.

Would you like to know more about the past?
Yes, sometimes I feel uncomfortable and dumb, especially around people like you who ask questions I can't answer.

What is an indian?
I have no problems when I come upon an *indian*.

How do you know someone is an indian?
Talking to someone who says he's an *indian,* someone
who can talk about *indian* problems.

How do people know you are an indian?
Well, first of all no one ever looks at me as an *indian.*
They say I'm Mexican or Italian, and I tell them, no, I'm
an *indian,* and they say, *really,* and I say, *yes.*

How do you define an indian?
I don't define it, I don't feel a need to define an *indian.*

Do you speak the indian *language?*
No, but I did once.

Do you want to know about the past?
I'd like to have it now, I carry part of it, but in today's
system I'm in step . . . you know the old folks on the
reservation seldom communicate to the kids about the
past.

What is the most serious problem the oshki anishinabe
face?
Unity and knowing who they are . . . finding out how
"white" other *indians* are, and what it means to live on
a reservation or in the city, or knowing who you can
trust. . . .

Why did you decide to go to college?
My mother decided for me.

Why do so many anishinabe *men marry white women?*
First you have to figure out what kind of *indian* marries a
white woman. Has the *indian* been raised on a reservation or in the city—they would have to be around white
people a lot to marry a white woman . . . a lot of people
say a person who marries a white is not an *indian,* but it

should be what you feel, love, and not have anything to do with being *indian*.

How can education be improved?
Both whites and *indians* have to learn about the *indian*. What good would it do for just the *indian* kid to learn about what happened to him in the past if the white kid don't know about it?

Ervin Sargent is the new coordinator of the proposed Urban American *indian* Center in the city. He was born on the White Earth Reservation and attended college for three years. He said more people are identifying as *oshki anishinabe* today because it has become a good thing to be this decade.

"In my generation we slumped down in our seats when the word *indian* was mentioned," said Sargent, who is married and the father of two children. His wife is *oshki anishinabe*. "I think in the next generation the young people will be more aware of the angles of identity and the invented things about being *indian* in the white society. . . .

"The *indians* who identify the strongest today are having trouble dealing with their identity when they marry white," he said, sitting in his office, "so they make special rules of identity in their organizations. . . .

"Some *indians* who don't have the pigment are recognized as *indian* by their names.

"But the identity thing is hard to understand," Sargent said, wrinkling his brow and folding his hands neatly. "Some white men know more about being *indian* than I do, because they have spent a long time talking to the old people. . . ."

Kent Smith was born on the White Earth Reservation and grew up in the town of Cass Lake on the Leech Lake Reservation. He is a soft-spoken sculptor and fine arts graduate from the University of Minnesota. His mother is white and his father is *oshki anishinabe* and an ordained minister. Smith said in high school he thought of himself as an *oshki anishinabe* person only in the sense of cultural and social deprivation.

"I haven't been told much about the past . . . there was very little discussion about *indian* culture in our family," he said, standing by his metal sculpture in his studio. "One day I came home from school and found this *indian* outfit on the wall and learned that my father was going to be in a parade . . . I was fourteen years old then and I started thinking about my culture. . . .

"I have never really had to be an *indian* because I wasn't brought up to be an *indian* . . . I was not brought up with a cultural awareness of the past, partly because I was never exposed to powwows and *indian* social events. . . .

"Trying to be an *indian* to me now would be the whole thing—the language and moving back to live on the reservation as an *indian*," he said, almost whispering; "the other level of being an *indian* would be to involve myself in the whole urban political and social thing. . . ."

White people seem to know more about what it

means to be an *indian* than the *oshki anishinabe* do because they have read the invented and standardized mythologies about the homogenized culture of the people. Most books that white people read about the *indian* are written by white people. When an *oshki anishinabe* goes to the library to learn about his past he finds that his past was interpreted by white historians and anthropologists. An interpretation of the past without dreams.

The tribal people in this nation have never forgotten that at the same time they were forbidden to speak their language and express their religion while living in poverty on colonial reservations, the federal government was subsidizing anthropologists and sociologists to study the people on the reservation and record what was being lost.

"Being an *indian* is being related to the people," said Lee Cook, who was born on the Red Lake Reservation. "It is the beautiful freedom to go back to the reservation—to the peace that is really mine."

3

Daydreaming
in a White School

He has noble impulses, and possesses in a high
degree the finer feelings and affections, and there is
no lack of evidence that he can be elevated and
highly civilized. . . .

—George Manypenny, commissioner of *indian* affairs,
1855

The footsteps of the *oshki anishinabe* women brushed
through the new snow past the black funeral hearse
waiting to carry the body of a fifteen-year-old *oshki
anishinabe* girl to her grave on the reservation.

She had committed suicide.

The door to the church opened and closed, raising
and lowering the mournful sound of the *oshki anishinabe* women wailing for the souls of all the *anishinabe*
dead.

The day before the funeral the principal of the Pine
Point elementary school on the White Earth reservation dismissed classes early in honor of the young girl
who had ended her life.

She had attended the reservation school through the seventh grade with other *oshki anishinabe* students from the community and then transferred to the high school in the white community off the reservation.

She had been frequently absent from the white school and might have dropped out if she had been old enough. Her friends and the white school counselors said she could not adjust to the alienation and cultural anxieties of attending a white school while living on the reservation.

More than half of the *oshki anishinabe* students who transfer from the all *anishinabe* school at Pine Point to the white public high school in Park Rapids, Minnesota, drop out before they graduate. The few *oshki anishinabe* who have graduated from the white school have bitter memories.

Paulette Fairbanks, who attended the Pine Point school on the reservation and then transferred to the high school in Park Rapids where she graduated with honors, said the most difficult transition she has ever made in her life was when she transferred from the reservation school to the white school.

"The transfer to college was easier for me," Paulette said, "than the transfer from Pine Point to Park Rapids. . . . It's the other way around with most white students—they have problems when they transfer to college."

After graduation from college, Paulette returned to the reservation to work with young *oshki anishinabe* students who would transfer as she did to the white high school.

Jerome Buckanaga, who also attended the reservation school and the white high school, returned to the reservation as principal of the Pine Point elementary school. He said he will never forget his feelings of alienation in the white school.

"I was scared when I first went to Park Rapids," he said, "but when the white kids kept pushing me around I fought back, and I fought hard. . . .

"After that they left me alone for the entire five years I was there . . . I told myself that I was an *indian* and I could do it better than the white, so I worked harder than they did, I put the screws on. . . . I could compete with the white students because I was better than they were. . . . Because I was better in sports they finally accepted me and pulled me in with them."

Buckanaga is a soft-spoken idealist who listens and acts more than he talks. He is married—his wife is *oshki anishinabe*—and has four children.

At the Park Rapids high school Buckanaga competed in basketball, baseball, football and track and reigned as homecoming king one year. He was also a competitive boxer and is still involved in a boxing program on the reservation.

His father worked as a handyman and laborer in the woods. Jerome followed two older brothers to college.

"I came back to the reservation because I wanted to change things," he said, sitting in the small library of the elementary school where he was a student. "This is *our* school and I want *our* people to look good here . . . I want this school to be an expression of the change and social conscience of the people. . . .

"When I went to school here all the teachers and the principal were white and their attitudes weren't much better than teachers off the reservation," he said, cradling his knee in his folded hands. "We want this to be an *indian* school with *indian* teachers in an *indian* environment so the students will know who they are when they transfer to white schools. . . ."

Twenty-five years ago only eight *oshki anishinabe* students graduated from high school in the entire state. About three hundred *oshki anishinabe* young people graduate from high school now, but still more than half of the estimated ten thousand *oshki anishinabe* students in public schools on the reservation and in the city leave school before graduating.

With the exception of the public high school on the Red Lake Reservation, students living on six different reservations in the state attend high school in white communities near the reservation, which means they are bussed to school from small *oshki anishinabe* communities.

Not only are the *oshki anishinabe* students alienated as minority people in racist educational institutions, but they are unable to participate in school and community activities after school hours. Their school day begins and ends on a school bus moving between the reservation and the dominant society.

The *oshki anishinabe* students living in the city face similar problems of alienation. A survey of *oshki anishinabe* students in the Minneapolis public schools conducted by the League of Women Voters found that of a population of thirteen hundred *oshki anishinabe* students only ten had graduated. Their dropout rate in the city is over 60 per cent. The overall dropout rate for students in the state—including the *oshki anishinabe*—is only 8 per cent—one of the lowest rates in the nation.

In an editorial in the *Minneapolis Tribune* the writer asked the white readers how they would react if more than half of their children were leaving school before they graduated. . . .

> The question is appropriate because that is just what is happening to *indian* students in this state. From half to sixty percent and more of the students don't stay long enough to get a high school diploma. . . .
>
> The scandal of *indian* education is now beginning to get the public attention it should have received long ago . . . but studies and criticism will accomplish nothing if public officials at the local and state level do not assume leadership on what is one of the most serious challenges to education today in the state. . . .

The dominant society would never accept that high a dropout rate among white students but public concern for the *oshki anishinabe* student was minimal until college-educated *oshki anishinabe* returned to the reservation and demanded changes in the educational system.

Few *oshki anishinabe* students in school today have parents who have graduated from high school and even fewer have parents or relatives who have attended college.

In the past the *anishinabe* were forced to attend

federal reservation boarding schools away from home where suppression of *anishinabe* culture and language and religion was the basic formula of education. Speaking the *anishinabe* language at a boarding school was forbidden, and young people were punished if they forgot and uttered a word of their language of songs and dreams. Federal agents on the reservation separated children from their parents in an effort to remove them from the *pagan influences* of woodland life and religion. The people were alienated from the very life style the dominant society now emulates.

The people have never forgotten the experiences of corporal punishment and manual labor at boarding schools.

Alexander Ramsey, an honorable white man in the history of the state a century ago, wrote the following about the *anishinabe* in this annual report on education: "Experience thus far confirms the opinion of most practical men in the *indian* country, that education and agricultural efforts can only hope for useful results when *indians* are removed in pursuance of treaties . . .

". . . and when manual-labor schools that will withdraw *their* children nearly entirely from *their* domestic influence, are exclusively established, under economical management, amongst them, to educate their rising generation in the arts, conveniences, and habits of civilization."

The "habits of civilization" have resulted in the education of young white liberals from isolated middle-class environments with buckled minds to teach *oshki anishinabe* children how to be proud of their past. Few *oshki anishinabe* students can speak the language of their grandparents and must now find a personal security in the distorted historical values taught in the white classrooms of the dominant society.

Three generations after Alexander Ramsey reflected on a racist solution to the *indian* problem, an *oshki anishinabe* girl quit school and left the reservation to live in the city.

"Before I moved here," she said, sitting in her apartment shared with another *oshki anishinabe* girl who had quit school, "I didn't look at myself as an *indian*, but not as a white either. Where I lived before, there were not too many people who cared for *indians*. They were not really abusive, but they didn't seem to think they were human. . . .

"In school," she said nervously, "the kids put me down, made me feel that being an *indian* was something to be ashamed of. Then I got to know *indians*. You feel at ease with them—you feel there is nothing wrong with being an *indian*. . . ."

Several years ago a presidential task force investigating education reported that public schools in the dominant society "do not view their task as that of helping *indian* children adjust to changes within their own culture, but to help them adjust to a culture alien to them. . . ."

This produces an emotional stress forcing an *oshki anishinabe* student to choose between contradictory sets of values and attitudes which, the task force found, "contributes to serious mental health problems, high dropout rates and unsatisfactory achievement levels. . . ."

The people have endured for a long time and they have remembered, and now they have the leaders who will carry out the demands of the people for justice and reparations.

Will Antell, director of *indian* education for the Minnesota Department of Education, testified before the Senate Subcommittee on *indian* education about the programs and problems of *anishinabe* education in the state. He explained that one priority of the Department of Education was to visit reservation communities and ask the people for the first time what they wanted changed in public education.

Antell was born in a two-room log and tar-paper shack on the White Earth Reservation. He attended reservation elementary schools and graduated from high school in Bagley, Minnesota. Graduating from Bemidji State College, Antell went on to complete his graduate work at Mankato State College in Minnesota. Before joining the Department of Education he taught for nine years in public schools in white communities.

After traveling on every reservation in the state talking to *oshki anishinabe* parents, Antell said he came to four general conclusions:

"The majority of *indians* have lost respect or confidence in the public schools and turning that around the schools have lost confidence in the people. . . .

"Secondly there was a distinct dissatisfaction with the curriculum in the public schools, in the fact that materials have depicted the people in an unfavorable light . . . the real story of our heritage was not being told in the classroom. . . .

"The parents thought that the institutions do not prepare teachers for teaching *indian* children . . . the institutions would not place teachers in *indian* schools for practice training.

"And the last thing I found was that there was a conflict in life style between the *indian* people and the dominant social group in the community where the public school was located. . . ."

Antell believes that the community should run the schools, and what the people want is what he will work to obtain. The people expressed dissatisfaction with library materials in the schools, so Antell obtained federal funds to establish an institute for school librarians to study and evaluate materials about the *anishinabe*, past and present.

Another program Antell is supervising is an educational administration program in the graduate school at the University of Minnesota. The one-year academic program will prepare *oshki anishinabe* college graduates and teachers to take positions of more responsibility in public school administration.

"When I talked to the parents it was like listening to my mother twenty years ago," Antell reminisced with bitterness in his voice. "I can remember times when we would come home from school and ask mother why others kids called us 'dirty *indians*.' . . .

"My mother could never really answer—she just trembled and the tears welled up in her eyes. . . . When

I talked to the mothers on my trip on the reservations I felt the same thing, but it seems more acute now than it was twenty years ago when I was in school," Antell said, sitting at his cluttered desk in the State Office Building.

"When I was young I rejected my *indian* ancestry because in the school I attended which was predominately white, I found out that it wasn't to my advantage to be an *indian*. . . .

"In a sense they assimilated me at a cost," he said. "I lost something in the heart, and it wasn't until I had a family that I fully realized what had happened. . . ."

Antell is an exceptional person in any culture, but what he remembers as an *oshki anishinabe* student in a white public school is not exceptional. It happens every day to almost every *oshki anishinabe* student. Not every student will express himself as well as Antell does but the feeling of alienation and degradation is the same.

Testifying before the Senate Subcommittee on *indian* Education, Antell was asked to comment on the efforts being made to improve curriculum and review text books which refer to the *oshki anishinabe* people.

"We have found Minnesota teachers very poorly informed about *indians* from our state. Naturally, this is also true of the *indians* themselves. In many cases they know even less about their history or identity. . . .

"There have been no attempts, to my knowledge, of intensive research on Minnesota *indians* by people of *indian* ancestry. Many of the older *indians* who possess an abundance of historical information are heading for the happy hunting ground, a part that history will never be able to record. We must act soon to preserve some of this information.

"The curriculum materials in school systems reflect a negative picture of the *indian*. Invariably he is something less than a human being, always depicted as lazy, a savage, massacring white people, on a warpath, drinking, and so forth. . . .

"Consider the impact on *indian* boys and girls as they read and observe materials such as this as they proceed through the public schools.

"We are in the process of massive curriculum changes for schools in Minnesota. Our major aim will be to include materials that will illustrate that American *indians* indeed have something to be proud of and that they can say with pride and dignity, I am an *indian*. . . ."

Antell is no idealist. He is hard-working and very practical. Some *oshki anishinabe* critics think he is too conservative at times, but most of the programs he has proposed from what the *oshki anishinabe* have wanted are in progress.

Without hesitation, Antell points out that in the past ten years the number of *oshki anishinabe* students graduating from high school has risen 200 per cent. The dropout rate, however, is still more than half of the *oshki anishinabe* students attending public schools.

"I was one of the first graduates from a state college on an *indian* scholarship," Antell said. "That was fifteen years ago . . . now there are about sixty

graduates from college each year . . . and more than
four hundred on the state scholarship program.''

With more *oshki anishinabe* students graduating
from high school and college, Antell pointed out, there
are more *oshki anishinabe* visible in professional oc-
cupations.

"When I was young it was not a good thing to be an
indian,'' he said with his hands clasped behind his
head; "a student would feel much better about being
indian if he could see more *indians* around. . . .

"And this is the responsibility of the teacher—to
make her class aware that there are successful *indians*
in all kinds of fields and to bring *indian* people into the
classroom.''

Very few of the certified *oshki anishinabe* teachers
are now teaching in the classroom. One reason is that
those certified to teach, and who have the experience,
have been offered better-paying professional jobs in
educational administration with greater responsibilities.

Antell taught for nine years and moved into administration. John Buckanaga taught on the White Earth
Reservation for several years and is now directing
community action programs. His brother Jerome
Buckanaga is principal of the Pine Point elementary
school, and a third brother, Charles Buckanaga, is a
teacher in the city public schools.

There are less than a dozen *oshki anishinabe* teachers in all the public schools in the state. In the past
most *oshki anishinabe* graduating from college were
certified to teach school. Now there is a shift in

academic interest among *oshki anishinabe* college students to sociology and psychology.

Ted Mahto, the *oshki anishinabe* poet and writer, has been working on curriculum revision for the public schools but his interests in education go far beyond curriculum. He is interested in identity through the use of symbolic *anishinabe* references from the tribal past. He is the *oshki anishinabe* poet and educator who thinks about the sentient meaning of the past in the lives of the people today.

"In the next few years we will see some innovative things in teaching *indian* children along the lines of visual expressions," Mahto said, holding his fingers to his forehead, "because there is a beautiful meaning in the passage of ideas through the stories the people told —the ability to tell a visual story—the words spoken between a father and son. . . .

"Some white teachers believe that *indians* just can't learn how to read well, but the people have the subskill of reading without knowing how to read through visual memories . . . through visual concepts—like day-dreaming—which is an area of education that is almost totally ignored. . . .

"I think we are going to have to learn in the public schools," Mahto said, smiling with his eyes, "to recognize the *indian* children who daydream as a very constructive kind of behavior, rather than to say he is not interested in working, you know; this kind of visual thinking is extremely important to everyone. . . .

"We are going to have to find ways to recognize what it is that is happening to a child when he daydreams, because this kind of visual thinking, you know, might be of more value with respect to learning how to live with one another than learning how to work a mathematical problem . . . there is something spontaneous and religious about visual thinking which is being ignored in the public schools. . . .''

Mahto was born on the Red Lake Reservation, attended federal boarding schools and several colleges and universities, earning a teaching certificate and a degree in German and English. He has taught German —also mathematics and physics—in reservation schools and in several white communities. He has two children who are in college. His son is interested in psychology and his daughter is studying medicine.

Mahto was fifteen years old when he graduated from boarding school and went to the West Coast to work in the shipyards until he was old enough to enlist in the service.

The only thing Mahto does more than smile is think. He likes to drink beer and talk with friends about poetry and the psychology of the unconscious. He is well read in many fields and has written several long poems and one unpublished novel.

He has always been a storyteller but he has not always been as serious about the meaning of education as he has become in the last few years. He sees *oshki anishinabe* identity as a possible matrix of mythologies invented by white people and real unconscious links to the tribal past. He believes that to understand the meaning of education for the *oshki anishinabe* the teacher must first understand the psychology of the people which is not derived from the popular histories of the people.

"There is very little behavior that we can be certain is only *anishinabe*," he said, lighting a cigarette, "because it has been so distorted by anthropologists trying to apply through their research the behavior of one tribe to another. . . .

"I still feel certain about sharing as *anishinabe* behavior, but in the urban center it hurts an *oshki anishinabe* to have this sharing behavior because he may have three kids to feed and along come his relatives from the reservation to care for while he is only scraping along. . . .

"Another thing is the *anishinabe* reverence for nature," Mahto said, gesturing with a fathomable extension of his arms. "I don't know about the other tribes, but I feel it is very strong with the *anishinabe*. . . . I see little kids sitting in the classroom looking at a bare branch or a flower . . . and I feel this reverence. . . .

"What has living in a small circular kind of shelter done over, say, two thousand years to the *anishinabe* unconscious," he asks himself, wrinkling his eyebrows and smiling. "I can remember my father saying something to my mother and maybe twenty minutes later she would answer. . . .

"Silence has so much meaning . . . there was no reason, you know, to shout or do violence to the language when living so close together.

"These are the things the people have never lost,

you know, they are part of the unconscious, they are part of the life meaning of the *oshki anishinabe* today. . . .

"The kind of life we led in a tribal society—and we are still part of some of that—was a very decent life because it had tremendous awe for the independence of another individual," Mahto said, stretching his legs out on the couch and adjusting a pillow under his head, "which is the kind of thing that some educators are discussing today—the education of the individual. . . ."

When Mahto finished his sentence he closed his eyes and fell asleep on the couch while his friends continued the conversation he had started. When he woke up he continued more or less where he had left off.

"We were talking about the education of the individual," he said, smiling.

4

Making It off the Reservation

Foot racing is much practiced, mostly however by the young people. Thus in early life they acquire an elasticity of limb as well as health of body, which are of priceless value to them in subsequent years. . . .

—George Copway, *anishinabe* missionary, 1850

Sitting in the back seat of a junked car in the tall grass next to the family two-room house on the reservation an *oshki anishinabe* youth holds in one hand the broken rear window handle and in the other hand the paw of his brown dog. In his morning dreams they fly through the autumn trees of his life color into a clear sky over the reservation

> my feathers
> sailing
> on the breeze

in the company of the good winds and crows and eagles of the past . . . below him on the green-and-

43

brown meadows the old men of the tribe look up from their long walks and wave six times in the six directions and smile . . . *you have the ribbons my grandson of the great spirit . . . you are one with the family of the crane . . . be moderate and remember the songs of the people . . .* the smiles of the old men are lost in the dust raised by the young reservation politicians swirling in their new cars on the dirt roads from vote to vote . . . it is time again for silent heroes . . . the grave houses below are crowded in rows between the pine trees . . . the public health nurse leaves the sagging shack of the *oshki anishinabe* woman who throws the wonder drugs in the trash

> I am as beautiful
> as the wild roses
> near the graves

and stays old and beautiful on herbs from the woodland . . . *return to the people* she whispers on the wind . . . *return to the people when you have the courage* . . . the sound of wailing voices trails off to the land of the sleeping sun and the trees never touch each other high in the wind . . . his dog licks his hand to loosen his grip and they soar too close to the tops of the century-old pines once free with the people . . . his mother will chant for him and place his picture in a frame . . . the family will tell stories to keep him strong and give him many good names to pass among the evil men of the world . . . below the lakes of the people are marked with fishing boats and tourist wakes

and the last grains of *manomin* . . . swooping on the
white schools and rows of pink and pale-green houses
he leaves the reservation for the city . . . his eyes
burn in the haze and his heart tightens through the
coarse names and rank epithets hanging over the city
like evil clouds . . . there was no thunder to fear only
the rage of machines building the end of the beginning
. . . his dog licks his hand again and they see the
people who preceded them never aimless on the
streets . . . one might have made philosophies and
told stories and been a teacher of the young . . . now
growing old in surplus military clothes he eases the
tribal past to rest on a park bench until a policeman
raps him with a stick to move . . . there is no place for
the past in the shape of breathing men . . . there is no
place for the wind . . . move . . . heroes of a forgotten
war . . . move . . . only the pigeon-stained statues of
white men will remain . . . go to work from this line the
white man has refused . . . wash these dishes . . . sort
these parts with your very dexterous *indian* fingers . . .
your beadwork is so beautiful . . . the men did nothing
in the past but gamble . . . be proud of your culture
. . . dirty *indian* . . . will you be my deer hunting
guide . . . when the squaws look good we leave for
home . . . blackdeer . . . downwind . . . bobolink . . .
frog . . . holenday . . . kingbird . . . what strange names
you people have . . . you must be a resident of the city
for one year before we can help you . . . the poor laws
of the state tell me so . . . fineday . . . is *fineday* one
word or two words . . . one word . . . what a beautiful
name . . . the invisible tribe . . . the only good *indian* is

a dead *indian* . . . what this country needs is a good *injun* tune up . . . use your *injunuity* . . . what does your dance mean . . . why do *indians* have blue eyes . . . beaulieu . . . carpenter . . . ellingworth . . . fairbanks . . . christianson . . . frenchman . . . will you show me around the reservation . . . my grandmother *was* an *indian* once . . .

"What are you doing?" his mother asked, bringing him down from his dreams and back to the reservation in a junk car behind the house.

"Nothing," he answered, looking out the window at the color of the trees across the road.

"Did something happen in school?"

"No."

"Names."

"No."

"The coach will be looking for you," his mother said, and slammed the door of the junk car. He was an athlete in a white high school and had missed the bus. The dust filtered down and settled on his dark eyelashes.

Not every *oshki anishinabe* youth who is a good athlete makes it in the white high school but athletics is one way to beat white people and win their tolerance and respect. Many *oshki anishinabe* college graduates were successful high school athletes—many won athletic scholarships to college.

William Lawrence, born on the Red Lake Reservation, and John Buckanaga, born on the White Earth Reservation, and Will Antell, born on the White Earth Reservation, and Ronald Libertus, born on the Leech

Lake Reservation, all attended white high schools and were outstanding athletes.

Lee Antell, brother of Will, was born on the White Earth Reservation, attended high school in Mahnomin, Minnesota, near the reservation and graduated from Moorhead State College. He was an outstanding athlete in high school and college.

"Athletics in high school helped me become socially acceptable to white people . . . I was from the reservation and my goal was to prove to myself that I could make it," Lee said. "Being an athlete was doing something for the school. . . .

"The kid from the reservation who doesn't have some talent useful to the image of the school has a tough time . . . when you're an athlete you are doing good things for the school image and get special attention from the coaches. . . .

"If I had been that kid in the classroom with no athletic ability I may not have made it—I would have been ignored in the school," Lee said, sitting in his office at the university.

Lee has taught for four years—two years in the high school he graduated from—and was director of a special library services program for librarians in *oshki anishinabe* schools in the state.

He says if an *oshki anishinabe* student from the reservation is a good athlete, the fact that he is *oshki anishinabe* makes little difference with the white students. He illustrates the special advantage of being important to the school as an athlete by comparing what happens when an athlete is absent from classes.

"The coach would come looking for me and ask me if everything was fine with me—he wanted to know if there was something he could do for me," Lee said. "The kids on the reservation who are truant are either forgotten or reported to the truant office—but not with the athletes who give the school a name."

Ervin Sargent, who was born on the White Earth Reservation, played basketball in high school. He has completed three years of college.

Ronald Libertus, who graduated from the University of Minnesota and has done graduate work in Russian literature and language, was outstanding in track and football while in high school. He received two scholarships—one athletic and one scholastic.

"Being an athlete is one way of making it off the reservation," Libertus said, scratching his head, "but I know good athletes who are still washing cars for a living . . . not everyone makes it just because he is an athlete."

Will Antell played football, basketball and participated in track in high school and received a college athletic scholarship for one year. He has completed graduate work in education and has taught physical education and coached in high school.

"When I was in high school they forgot about my being an *indian* because I was their local hero," Will said. "I have always been critical of this school because of what happened. . . ."

Francis Brun, who was born on the Red Lake Reservation where he now lives with his family and owns the only automatic laundromat on the reservation, played basketball on the reservation high school team. The year he played, the team won the state regional basketball tournament.

John Buckanaga set the mile track record in high school and was captain of the baseball and track teams. He was an outstanding high school athlete from the reservation. When he returned to the White Earth Reservation to teach school he was also a recreational and athletic coach.

One of the most outstanding *oshki anishinabe* athletes in the history of the state is Henry Boucha, who played hockey for the high school in Warroad, Minnesota, and led his team to the state hockey tournament.

Boucha turned down an athletic scholarship to the University of Minnesota to play with the Winnipeg Jets in the Western Canadian Junior League on a two-year contract.

He had wanted to play professional hockey all his life and decided not to attend college because he would be too far from his dream and his family.

"I'm also glad that I went with the Canada team instead of going on to college," Boucha said in Minneapolis after playing for the United States Nationals. "It's a much tougher league and they hit a lot harder than they did in high school, but I like it. . . ."

He first played hockey in kindergarten but has also played football and baseball in high school. He has always been successful in competitive sports. When he graduated from high school he was considered one of the most outstanding individual hockey players in the history of the state.

Boucha is the son of a commercial fisherman. His mother has worked in a hospital kitchen for fifteen years to help care for her children and two orphaned grandchildren.

"Henry earned what he got through hard work," his mother said of her *oshki anishinabe* son, who has become a legend among hockey fans in the state, "not because he is a minority."

5

Keeping the Family Together

brave old woman
defending her children
she endured
fighting for us all

—*anishinabe* song poem

In the traditional past the women of the tribe gathered the wild rice, berries, and wood for the fire, and tanned the hides and dressed the skins, prepared the food, dried the fish and cut birch bark and built the wigwam for the family.

The *anishinabe* women who once learned the secrets of herbal medicine and participated in the *midewiwin*—the sacred religion of the people—now teach school, administrate poverty programs, serve on boards and commissions, attend college and are militants in the causes of human and civil rights on the reservation and in the city.

The *oshki anishinabe* women of today live in large

51

urban centers, small towns and on the reservation.

The life style of the people has changed but the endurance and courage of the *anishinabe* woman has never changed—it has grown stronger with time.

A male *oshki anishinabe* public school administrator said that in the old days it took four women and two men to build a birch bark canoe—the men shaped the wood and the women prepared the bark and pitch to hold it together.

"Nothing has changed," he said, smiling with affection. "It still takes four women and two men to run a program—the life style is different, but the spirit is the same."

"An important driving force behind the *indian* education movement is the *anishinabe* woman," said Rosemary Christensen, *oshki anishinabe* mother of two boys, educator, writer, lecturer and scholar, "her perceptions, her labors and her strong commitment to the education of her children."

The honored role of women in the new world of the people is as strong as it was in the past. While men yield to her courage, the *oshki anishinabe* woman understands the insecurities and special needs of *oshki anishinabe* men and she strengthens their masculine identity in a complex and changing world.

"We are a beautiful people," said Esther *Nahgah-nub*, who works in the American *indian* Fellowship Association in Duluth, Minnesota, "and I thrive on being *indian*."

"Our *indian* women have been *deindianized* . . . our whole *chippewa* nation has to be *reindianized*," she said with her hands folded beneath her chin. "We have been *deindianized* . . . we have no religion, no language, no culture, no tribal dress; everything that we are was stifled by the white people . . .

"But it is still here," she whispered, tapping her heart with her hand, "the beauty that is us will be brought out again through the heart."

Esther is divorced and has two children. She was born in Superior, Wisconsin, attended college for one year and became a branch manager for an insurance company. She left a good-paying job "among the white people" to work with her own people at the fellowship center, and at that time began using the last name *Nahgahnub*. She plans legal action to make the name official.

"I come from a long line of chiefs," she said, raising her eyebrows and hands in sacred reference to the *anishinabe* past, "and I want to be known now as *Nahgahnub*."

Nahgahnub—which means *feather end*, according to William Warren in his *History of the Ojibways*—was a hereditary chief of the Mille Lacs band of the people. He was of mixed *anishinabe* and *dakota* ancestry and a member of the *maingan odem*—the wolf family.

Esther *Nahgahnub* listens for hours to the old *anishinabe* people telling their tales of the past. She studies the language and punctuates her speech with *anishinabe* words, but not all *oshki anishinabe* are as intense about returning to the past.

When asked what it means to be an *oshki anishinabe* woman, Paulette Fairbanks responded, "The people have too many moods from one day to the next to capture any one of them for a definite answer. . . .

"No one ever comes up with an answer," she said. "You can say it is a way of life. Being an *indian* woman comes out in my attitudes because I see things in common with other *indian* people—like humor, life experiences on the reservation, commodity foods, the public health nurse, but not everything is grim in humor. There are experiences held in common that make one feel like an *indian*."

Paulette was born at home at Pine Point on the White Earth Reservation. She attended reservation elementary school and high school in a white community where she graduated with honors. She earned a degree in French and English from the University of Minnesota.

Paulette has completed work on a graduate degree in sociology at the University of Atlanta while working as a management specialist for training programs on several reservations in the southeast United States.

Claricy Smith was born on the White Earth Reservation and grew up in Cass Lake on the Leech Lake Reservation. She has had different experiences as an *oshki anishinabe* woman.

She graduated from high school at Saint Mary's Hall, a private Episcopal school for girls, and earned her college degree in humanities from the University of Minnesota.

Claricy has been a service worker with the American *indian* Employment Center in the city, and has been employed as an education specialist for Upward

Bound programs under the Department of Health, Education and Welfare. She spends most of her time traveling in a dozen states supervising programs for reservation young people.

"I really don't know what it means to be an *indian* woman," she commented. "I don't really have the feeling in the city that people around me are concerned about my being *indian*. . . .

"The whole thing of who I am in terms of being an *indian* is a late thing for me. Until I was about sixteen, everything and everyone around me, including my parents, were saying in a covert sense that *white* is right."

Her mother is white and her father is an ordained *oshki anishinabe* Episcopal minister in Cass Lake where the family has lived since Claricy and her brother, Kent, a sculptor and fine arts college graduate, first attended school. While her father has been very active in civil rights and human rights organizations and programs in the state for *oshki anishinabe* people for more than twenty years, the family has not lived on the reservation.

Claricy spends her free time in her comfortable apartment reading and writing poetry and attending art exhibits. She listens to tribal music less often than classical and rock recordings.

Bonnie Wallace was born on the Fond du Lac Reservation but has spent much of her life working in the city.

Most recently she has been active in the American *indian* Movement in the city, which is the most militant *oshki anishinabe* organization in the state.

"I get static all the time about my light skin," she said, looking down at her small hands. "The militants tell me that I don't look right or that I don't dress right —they're on a thing about fullbloods now, and if you have light skin, well, forget it."

"They want dark skin now, but they only stereotype themselves and everyone else," she said. "I was born on the reservation and I feel like an *oshki anishinabe* woman because I have lived that way and I remember my grandmother telling me to be proud. . . .

"I look at skin color about like wearing buckskin dresses and feathers in my hair to show everyone that I'm the great *indian*," Bonnie said, squeezing her hands together and then rubbing her arms as if she were cold. "I don't need racists no matter what color they are."

When members of the American *indian* Movement occupied the offices of the area director of the Bureau of *indian* Affairs in Minneapolis demanding more jobs and meaningful programs, Bonnie was told by militant leaders to leave the room while the television cameras were there because the militants did not want her light face tones shown on television news reports.

"The whole thing was my skin color," she said bitterly. "They want me around to think about things and do the paperwork but they don't want me to be seen on television."

Bonnie has worked in employment and educational programs for the *oshki anishinabe* people both on the reservation and in the city. She has eight brothers and sisters and graduated from high school while living on the reservation.

"Being an *indian* woman is inside," she said, touching her chest. "I just ignore all the static about my color." Bonnie believes that the most serious problem young *oshki anishinabe* have to face is their identity.

"*Indians* just don't know who they are or where they are . . . nothing but the identity thing," she said, shaking her head, "trying to keep up with the cultural thing, you know. But again we have our leaders who think about the color of skin and don't know how to speak the *indian* language, which I think is really funny. . . .

"We are just floating, floating, many people don't know if they should get hung up on the cultural thing or move forward. We are just floating. . . .

"As far as women leaders go, I just don't think there really are any, and if the few who say they are had a good husband they wouldn't be quite so active all the time. . . ."

Esther *Nahgahnub* refers to the tribal past to give meaning to her experiences in the present. She is moved by the music and language and religion of the past.

Tears come to her eyes when she sees an *oshki anishinabe* man who has been drinking and walks alone through the city streets at night. These men walk in legendary elegance.

"I know men who feel they can only be an *indian* when they are drunk," Esther said, her voice trembling. "Is this the product of boarding schools or the white society, that a man is ashamed to show his heart?

"I have seen young men who could only sing from their *indian* soul when they are drunk. What has happened to our prayer?" she asked, and then answered, "our *indian* dance is a prayer. It is not like the dance of the white people.

"Our men are born leaders," she said, her hands gesturing, "and I believe the *indian* woman should stand in back. The man should get the glory and recognition . . . but men aren't doing that now, they have lost their pride . . . the women once held the tribe together while the men were out hunting, and I think the women are doing sort of the same thing today— they are holding their people together while the spirit is being reborn.

"Once an *indian* man has his pride again his spirit is reborn and the *indian* woman can go back into the background where she should be, because the man has always been superior and he always will be the spiritual strength of the tribe."

She explains that *anishinabe* music and religion is the way a man finds his soul and spirit and pride. She has profound respect for the man at the drum during a ceremonial dance. "The drum is the way of worshiping for the man and it is his way of speaking with his soul for the woman," she said.

Esther told a story about a young militant woman at a ceremonial dance who sat down at the drum and picked up the drumstick. "I screamed across the room, *don't touch that* to the woman, and she looked up. When I went over I told her that if a woman takes the drumstick she takes the place of the man and strips him of his soul and pride,'' she said, reanimating the story with her hands and eyes.

''She understood what I said, because she knew that the drum is the way a man worships.''

Esther respects the place of men but believes the woman should push the man because ''Right now our men are not sure of themselves . . . I think our men are very militant if they can be drawn out and respected by women.''

Esther said she has not dated a white man for several years because she has more love for the *oshki anishinabe* man. She believes the place for the woman is behind the man because he needs more support now than he has ever needed to reestablish the pride of the people.

About a century ago the tales about the customs of the *anishinabe* told by a ninety-year-old member of the *midewiwin* were printed in *The Progress*—a newspaper published on the White Earth Reservation about the turn of the last century. The old *anishinabe* was speaking to his grandchildren about the courtship and marriage customs of the people:

My *nojishe,* you ask me if there was any jealousy in those days. Well, it was as it is today, only the spite was perhaps more bitter and the revengeful feelings more severe than it is now. It was no uncommon occurrence among the women for a wife or rival crazed with love and jealous frenzy to seek an early opportunity to viciously attack the object of her hatred and if possible cut off her nose or her braids of hair—the former object being to

disfigure the face and the latter to disgrace the victim.
Among the men death was often the result of rivalry in
love affairs. . . .

The thoughts of the old man are not the thoughts of
many *oshki anishinabe* today. Few would welcome the
intensity of the tribal past when out of jealousy a
woman could lose her hair or nose. Today *oshki
anishinabe* women have different views about their
interpersonal relationships with *oshki anishinabe* men,
but most agree that they have more meaningful
relationships with *oshki anishinabe* men than with
white men.

"There is absolutely no comparison between an
indian man and a white man," Esther *Nahgahnub*
emphasizes, "because white people have to possess
everything, even white women have to possess their
men. . . .

"I have had no dates with white men for about ten
years," she said, adding that she did not think she
would ever date a white man again.

Bonnie Wallace prefers to date *oshki anishinabe*
men because she feels she understands the meaning of
the relationship better than with a white man. White
men always find it necessary, she said, to ask me
"What's it like to be an *indian*? . . ."

"But *indian* men are very possessive," Bonnie
emphasized. "I don't know why, maybe because they
aren't as secure in the world as other men . . . one
thing is certain, though, when you're out with an

indian man you are out with him *only* and can't look at another man . . . you are his woman.''

Both Claricy Smith and Paulette Fairbanks have dated *oshki anishinabe* men, or men from other tribal cultures, more often than white men. They agree that it is easier to communicate with a man who has had similar experiences in life.

"I have dated more *indian* fellows and have had relationships that have lasted longer than with white people,'' Paulette said. "I think it's the common experiences—but much depends on the person.''

"In terms of a personal relationship I do feel more comfortable dating an *indian* man,'' Claricy said, "but for a long time I had an identity problem as an *indian* woman relating to *indian* men . . . I always felt tougher than they were—I don't think that was true, but it was my feeling when I was younger.''

Traditionally, *anishinabe* women have been sensitive and protective mothers. Many *oshki anishinabe* draw from the tribal past things which complement the good feelings of the present. One tribal feeling which is as true today as it was hundreds of years ago is the protective warmth the *oshki anishinabe* mother feels for her children and family.

The *oshki anishinabe* mother does even more today for the family than she did in the tribal past. She once cut the wood and gathered the wild rice and built the wigwam. Now she cares for the family and serves on commissions and committees to better the community and the education of the young—and when she gets angry about an injustice to her family she will demand changes in the strongest voice. The most militant of men will yield to an angry *oshki anishinabe* woman.

There is much tenderness in the *oshki anishinabe* family—and there are problems as there are in any other family in the world—but the *oshki anishinabe* have the strength from the collective memory of the tribal past to give more meaning to their lives in the present.

My *nojishe,* you want to know now about our marriage customs [the old *anishinabe* man told his grandchildren a century ago]. My people wore no dress but that made from the furs and skins of animals slain in the chase, and there were many very handsome women and men. A young man would . . . soon see some young woman who would impress him very much. He would then go on a hunt and select some fine furs and skins, which he would carry to the wigwam of the young girl to make her dresses to adorn her person, and if she accepted his attentions she would in return make him something whereby to adorn his person also, which was generally a handsome pair of moccasins . . . the young *anishinabe* woman . . . would then . . . cut wood which she would carry on her back and take it to the wigwam of his parents. . . . If there were no objections, his mother would come out and in a gentle manner would proceed to pinch or blow the nose of the young woman as a token that she was welcome as one of the family. Then, after the lapse of ten days . . . the young couple would again meet together, and the man would take the hand of his bride and say: "We must live for one another, we must be true and live together until we die." They were then looked upon as man and wife.

The marriage customs of the past are not so difficult to relate to the present. Reading the tales of the old man, a few *oshki anishinabe* have taken up the pleasure of pinching noses to show affection.

The *oshki anishinabe* enjoy the humor of their own human folly and foolishness, but they despise with a vengeance those white men who tour the reservation and write about the lives of the people and the meaning of the family on the reservation.

"I grew up on the reservation," said Pearle Fabre, who was the elected secretary-treasurer of the White Earth Reservation Business Committee, "and my association as an *indian* is that *indians* have far deeper relationships within the family than a white observer will ever see. . . .

"If studies must be done," she said, "then the *indians* should get the money to study the white people, who seem to have more family problems than any people in the world."

More believable than white sociologists advancing personal academic careers are the many men who look back on their *oshki anishinabe* families as the source of strength to overcome the problems of living in a white society.

Many *oshki anishinabe* men who hold responsible positions in education and public service attribute their success in life to a strong mother who kept the family together in the midst of poverty and racism. It is not uncommon to hear an *oshki anishinabe* college-educated man say that if it were not for his mother he would not have succeeded in the dominant society.

White people may share the same sentiments, but the real difference is that an *oshki anishinabe* man can strengthen the meaning of the family through the collective memory of the tribal past—the tribal past that many young white people are trying to find to give meaning to white lives.

"*Indian* mothers in the past thirty years have done the job of keeping the family together," said Ted Mahto, teacher, father, poet, and former public school administrator.

John Buckanaga, a graduate of Bemidji State College and former elementary school teacher on the White Earth Reservation where he was born, said his mother was "the one who held the family together. She provided us with good discipline—we had a mother who was strong."

Will Antell said, "The force in my life was my mother . . . she was the most inspiration that I ever had. She worked hard all her life to see us through school."

The *oshki anishinabe* mothers have had the courage and pride to carry the dreams that their sons would free the people of the tribe from fear and hopelessness to live a better life. And the sons are teachers, health administrators, tribal officials, mechanics, writers, orators, sculptors, militants and dreamers.

6

Dreams in the Fourth Dimension

If you wish to know me you must seek me in the clouds

I am a bird who rises from the earth and flies
far up into the skies out of human sight

though not visible to the eye my voice is heard from afar
and resounds over the earth

—Keeshkemun, nineteenth century *anishinabe* orator

Jumping out of his chair with a cigarette stuck between two fingers of his left hand, Ted Mahto began to lecture: "I have heard anthropologists remark that the tribal world view was a smaller circle of things than that of the white man," he said, walking in a circle, "but I have a suspicion that the *indian* had a closer feeling of his environment than the white man, who was always measuring and weighing everything in terms of what gave him a greater aesthetic sense. . . ."

Ted Mahto is a happy and a lonely man because he feels every minute the pain and joy and rage of having dark skin in a white society—and he is lonely because he thinks so much about *oshki anishinabe* youth and the injustices of modern education.

He has been a school administrator, teacher, writer, father, poet and a fine storyteller. When he read his unpublished poem *Uncle Tomahawk* to a group of Junior League women in Duluth, there were whispers among the wives of professional men that the poem violated the mythological sanctions of the *noble savage*. Mahto read his poem in a conversational tone.

UNCLE TOMAHAWK

When I was just this side of papoose,
I saw my father
kick my pregnant mother
And later on they told me
one of two had lived
And that my mother died also.

'n somebody pushed me out in
front of some long stern faces
And asked me to tell them what
I had seen. 'n I cried.

Then my father ran across
the room and picked me up
And cried and hugged me
and said, "Someday, you'll—"

They took him away
'n 'nay sent us to *indian* School,
me and my brother and sister.

Some guy smashed my mouth
the first day we were there.
'n they smashed me every day
until I learned to like it.

And I spent a lot of my life
tryin' to get people to smash me in
the mouth.

I guess what I never learned to
like was watchin' them smash my
little brother.
Cause I knew he'd never learn to
like it.
And I was right.

Some guy called him a dumb *indian*
and he piled into the back end of a truck
goin' one hundred miles an hour with
his brain drowned in alcohol.

'n I kept on lookin' for guys to
smash me in the mouth, 'n found
a place where there were experts at mouth
smashin'.

'n finally I graduated and they
said, "Now you'll have to stop lookin'
and do some smashin'."

So I became a teacher.

You said, "What do you want for
Christmas?" and I said, "Peace," and
you sent me $5.00.

I said, "Why me?" And you said, "I'd
rather fornicate with *indians*." And I said,
"Why?" And you said, "*Indians* aren't as bad.
If I gotta relate to minorities, I'd rather do it
with *indians*."

I said, "A lotta my people are starving."
And you said, "Why the hell don't they
go to work and work their way up like
I did?"

I took my half-*indian*-half-white son
to an *indian* meeting and they said, "Shit,
he's not *indian*." So, I took him to a
meeting of blacks and whites and they said,
"He's *indian* and won't be able to relate to
us." So I took him down to the river
and cut him up and threw him away, 'cause
what the hell good is a guy without
a thing to identify with.

The grass keeps growin'—taller!
But reservations keep growin'—smaller!
And, really, how long is that?

Beauty, truth, and love are solutions as long
as we don't abuse one for the other.
I said, "I love you," and you said,
"Let me think about that awhile!"

I was standing along a road sorta out of
town with my thumb out, try 'na get a ride,
and you stopped and got out and beat
the hell outa me with a tire chain till I almost died.

An' in the hospital the sheriff said,
"One 'nem guys is the mayor's son
'n they ain't a thing I can do, Boy!"

"But I'm an educated *indian,*" I said.
So—He took out a knife, cut out my heart,
and said, "It's still an *indian* heart 'sfar
as I can see."

Ted Mahto moves through time in the *anishinabe* spirit like a bishop on an evening walk, reluming his experiences of the present through the conscience of the *anishinabe* past. He is a metaphorical speaker and listener, showing that the past and the present have the same rhythm in stories about people.

The *oshki anishinabe* writer is a visual thinker soaring on the rhythms of the woodland past through the gestures of the present—he is a poet, an autobiographer, a storyteller, an essayist, a public speaker and an epistler. The *oshki anishinabe* creative writer dreams in the fourth dimension of time and lives everywhere.

In the past the tales of the *anishinabe* were not an objective collection of facts. The *oshki anishinabe* writer tells stories now as in the past—stories about people, not facts. The ideas and visions can be seen more in human gestures than in words. Stories are a circle of believable dreams and oratorical gestures showing the meaning between the present and the past in the life of the people. The stories change as the people change because people, not facts, are the center of the *anishinabe* world.

"When the great spirit made up his mind to create man he took a handful of earth and rubbed it together in his palms [the old *anishinabe* leader of the *midewiwin* told his grandchildren a century ago], and a man was formed. . . . The spirit below the earth who was a very imposing spirit, with heavy locks of white hair, said to the great spirit in council: *What are you going to do with only one* anishinabe?

"In answer to this question the great spirit took another handful of earth and rubbed it in his palm and a woman was formed. Then he said: *This person shall be the fruit of the earth and the seed from which shall come the* anishinabe *people*. This, my grandson, is how the *anishinabe* originated and became so numerous."

If Mahto had lived more than a century ago he would have been capable of telling the same story of the origin of the *anishinabe*, and when he had finished, he would have laughed and hugged the listeners, his grandchildren, the *anishinabe*, and they would have been strong and laughed together.

In an unpublished novel, Mahto wrote about his principal character, Moses Two Crow, a family man and decorated war hero, as if he were looming out of the past in legendary elegance:

He walked with an effortless ease into the sun that streamed from the east into his face. The bright color of his sienna skin, soft and finely textured, reflected the sun in a faintly reddish brown glow.

Yet, nothing of his personal appearance was conspicuous. . . . No, it was not his appearance that caused people, even at this early hour, to turn and watch this young, handsome, neatly dressed, red giant move up the street. It was his walk. One could have said that he was born to walk. It was a walk that seemed to spring, not from his calves or thighs or the balls of his feet, not from the very slight swing of his arms, but from his whole body, and it had with it something of an apology whenever he walked among his white brothers as if he were actually sorry to display a skill which they could never master. . . .

This seemed to be the source of the pleasant little grin he showed to people as he passed on the street. It was a grin which asked forgiveness of those far less endowed than he; a grin, humble in its character, and presented with dignity not insolence. Too, there was really something of shame as if he sensed that he, in his simplicity, had caused the evil envy on the faces of the onlookers. . . .

Mahto writes and tells stories among his *oshki anishinabe* friends like Moses Two Crow walks. The more the world hears the *oshki anishinabe* voice in humor and poetry and stories the more the white man will be left alone forever with his *evil envy*.

Gabe Kangi, another character in Mahto's unpublished novel, is talking with his friends in a restaurant about the meaning of being an *indian* in the white dominant society :

What is it about the white man that makes him think everybody wants to live like him? First he trampled the hell out of us, then he turned around and tried to buy us off to salve his own conscience. But then we're using hindsight again. If all we can do is look back, then the *indian* is dead. And for all practical purposes (and western man likes to think he's very practical) maybe we're better off dead.

If their psychology doesn't apply to us, if their capitalism is incomprehensible to us, if their ideals like charity and love and virtue are not what we place in highest esteem, how can we ever really fit?

White men unfamiliar with the *oshki anishinabe* may believe that the characters are only fictional—but every day of the week the people gather in restaurants to talk about where they are in the paradoxical world of the white man—just like Moses Two Crow and Gabe Kangi.

"We have to teach white people how to be *real indians* in the urban center," Mahto said, smiling, "so they will leave *indians* alone . . . if we write enough maybe we can keep the white man home reading so he will leave us alone. . . ."

The situations of most stories told and written by the *oshki anishinabe* are real experiences. The tension only suggests the pathos and humor, leaving the listener to complete the story.

James Sayers, who lives in Ponemah on the Red Lake Reservation, illustrates *oshki anishinabe* humor —that metaphorical tension few white people understand but respectfully laugh about anyway—with the following story:

An *oshki anishinabe* widow living on the reservation left her small house one afternoon to visit with her friends in a house down the road.

While she was gone her house filled with smoke from

an overheated stove and started to burn. Two *oshki anishinabe* boys playing nearby saw the smoke and flames and ran to the house where the old woman was visiting to tell her that her house was burning down.

When they rushed through the door breathless and excited and told the old woman about her house she turned slowly toward them, smiled, slapped her protruding stomach with one hand, and said—everything is all right because I have the key right here—and then slapped her stomach again and laughed.

Sometimes the people laugh more about the subjects of *oshki anishinabe* humor than at the stories they find time to tell. Mentioning *oshki anishinabe* humor turns thoughts into collective visual experiences: Do you remember commodity peanut butter sticking to the roof of your mouth . . . The smell of pinto beans and bear grease and an earthen crock of good things fermenting in the corner of the house . . . Or the public health nurse wrinkling from the fingertips when she just happened to stop by and check heads for lice . . . Or blond VISTA workers running home before dark to tell courageous stories about living on a dirt floor in a little house on the reservation . . . Or white women on a bus tour of the reservation asking a tribal leader what his women do when they run out of breast milk and the leader answering after a long stoical pause that the reservation braves milk porcupines to keep the children alive and the white women being relieved with that information . . . Or do you remember sleeping with your dog in a junked car parked beside your house on the reservation and dreaming of the time you will hurtle down the dirt roads of the world and return one clear day a rich and decorated hero . . .

"Soon there will be a number of *indian* humorists on the stage," Ted Mahto predicted. "They will come in this decade when the people are more able to laugh about their common experiences with white people—when they are more secure about their identity."

Mahto smiled and after a long pause he told a story about *oshki anishinabe* people participating in committee meetings on the reservation. The anthropologists, he said, explain that the people are very democratic—everyone gets a chance to speak at a meeting. "I remember an old man at a meeting on the reservation who, when he was recognized by the chairman and told that he had the floor, stood up, looked around and said, 'Mister chairman, I would like to make a commotion . . .' "

Ronald Libertus, *oshki anishinabe* director of community programs for the Minneapolis Institute of Arts, believes that "*indian* humor will emerge as public entertainment when the ramifications of hate are more clearly known, as is true with black humorists."

The language of the *oshki anishinabe* makes a difference in the special sense of humor the people have—the language is visual and more closely related to what the people feel and believe.

"That symbolizing process that Western man has become so adept at," Mahto explained, "is not true with tribal languages because tribal languages carry more feeling. Modern languages have abandoned the feeling for information and fact . . . the independent information about technology in the language of the dominant society is reflected in tribal linguistic thoughts as visual feelings.''

The *anishinabe* language of the past was a language of verbal forms and word images. The spoken feeling of the language—and thought processes—is a moving image of tribal woodland life. The visual images are not static or inferred from logic. The language of the people is descriptive, euphonious, and a sympathy of cosmic rhythms and tribal instincts, memories and dream songs, expressing the contrasts of life and death, day and night, man and woman, courage and fear.

Mahto believes these visual qualities in the language are not lost when an *oshki anishinabe* speaks only English.

''I tend to be somewhat prejudiced in this view, that an *indian* who feels free and at ease on a reservation is much more alive and aware of things around him than the person in the dominant society who must know how far it is from here to there and define things in structured terms and stereotypes without visual feeling.''

After a long pause Mahto smiled again and said he wanted to tell a personal story that shows how he was caught between the sensitivities of visual dreams and the structural social thinking of the white listeners:

''The morning after Martin Luther King led his first peaceful march in the South, I was a teacher in a white school, and that morning I was kind of excited about what had happened . . . I felt a certain kinship with another minority group who were doing their thing without violence. . . .

"So that morning when I arrived at school I went down to the boiler room where the men gathered before class for the first smoke and, feeling good, I rushed into the boiler room where all the white teachers were sitting—I was the only *indian* there—and said jokingly: *All right you bastards, the* indians *are next. We're gathering guns and storing them on the reservations, but first we plan to march peacefully on you bastards. . . ."*

Mahto laughed hard when he saw their faces in his story and then continued: "And one of the teachers said to me after a long pause, *You won't get past the municipal liquor store . . .* he shut me up for a couple of weeks and I stayed out of the boiler room for longer than that. . . .

"I don't understand Western man sometimes," he continued the thought. "I feel that the *anishinabe* and the *dakota* and other tribes entered into a conflict with the white man on a very noble and honorable basis —to fight for my land and the freedom of the tribal people . . . and my children and family—a very noble reason to fight. And after it was over men should say, we fought a hell of a battle didn't we . . . you won and I lost. . . .

"The assumption I feel is that this put us on a good ground with the values of the white man, but it didn't, it was nothing like that at all. Instead it was degradation and humiliation, and *we beat you bastards,* the white man goes on saying, you know ..." he said, pacing back and forth with his hands poised at his chest. "And the reason we beat you, the white man goes on saying, is because we are superior to you ... superior to *me*. ...

"We face the same thing in the so-called war on poverty and in education and jobs and everywhere ... the white man saying *we are superior to you* ... but there is still that envy of tribal people."

The *oshki anishinabe* tell about their experiences more often in letters, and autobiographical narratives, and in speeches and verbal stories, than they do in short stories and poems and novels. The speeches and narratives are usually very serious because they are most often addressed to white people and deal with the political, economic and educational aspirations of the people.

George Mitchell, a rugged activist born on the White Earth Reservation, was the first *oshki anishinabe* to run in the aldermanic elections in Minneapolis. He was a candidate in a ward where the largest number of *oshki anishinabe* people live. He lost the election but his identity caused *oshki anishinabe* voters to argue more about their representatives on the city council. The media equal-time sanction for political candidates brought the *oshki anishinabe* in the urban center to public attention.

In one of his campaign speeches to a large group of citizens, Mitchell opened with one of his favorite remarks to ease the tension. After a long and nervous pause, while he looked around the audience, he took the microphone and said: *Now I know how Custer felt . . .*

"I will admit that I am a bitter man," he went on, his lips trembling, "bitter because while driving here tonight I see the same things I saw ten years ago. Muddy roads that remind me of things similar or worse than those on the reservation, condemned houses, well-lighted liquor stores and poorly lighted streets. . . .

"Who knows more about these conditions than the people who live here? We have heard for a long time how government is for the people, but how can a government without the people be for the people? . . .

"Think about that child who drowned in a condemned building. The city government said that they were not responsible. Think about that boy who was shot in the back of the head by a police officer. His death was justified on official paper. Think about where your children are playing tonight—poorly lighted parks, million-dollar construction sites, muddy streets or abandoned buildings that still stand to remind us we are poor. . . .

"We have been studied often enough by researchers. Had these studies been conducted with good faith instead of selfish motives, our needs and concerns would not exist today. We have been planned for and protected by the government but not with our sentiments.

"I feel and believe that it is less of a problem to be poor than to be dishonest. . . .

"We have heard a great deal about federal money for demonstration cities but little from people who will live in them—are we to become demonstration people?...

"We have come here with broad minds and slim waists and let us hope these do not change places in the days to come...."

The audience applauded and Mitchell received a total of sixty-eight votes in the election. Very few *oshki anishinabe* were registered to vote. The winner was white and received more than a thousand votes.

The expression of *oshki anishinabe* visual experiences is presented in many different literary forms— the anecdote and archetypal stories from the collective unconscious of the tribal past, the sermon of conscience and identity, the stories of folly, short narrations of humorous and tragic incidents, the epistle, poetry, the novel and the short story. The *oshki anishinabe* knows what he is writing about because he sees what he is saying.

7

The People Are Afraid of Change

It is not necessary to detail each and every wrong
that my poor people have suffered . . .
the white men have been like greedy lions,
they have driven us from our nation, our homes,
and possessions . . . to seek refuge . . .
among strangers . . .

—George Copway, *anishinabe* missionary, 1847

The *oshki anishinabe* politician may be one of the most
complex human beings in the history of man. At the
same time he is liberal with the young people, he is
conservative in the *anishinabe* language of the old
people—his rhetoric soaring on the breath of the tribal
past and tacking on the new winds that draw the
most votes.

Most *oshki anishinabe* politicians spend about as
much time talking with white government officials as
they do to the people on the reservation. In the tribal
past a man of good life and experience had the
independent liberty to make decisions for himself and
his family, but he was not elected to serve four years

with unspecified political powers. Today the *oshki anishinabe* politician is elected by popular vote on the reservations and he is expected to win favors from the federal government for the betterment of the reservation.

The *oshki anishinabe* politician is a useful mythological figure for white politicians to be seen with during election time. In the liberal mentality a white candidate for a federal public office is immediately recognized as a humanitarian when he is pictured standing next to some tribal leader in traditional buckskin and headdress.

Many white politicians have been adopted by the tribes and given *indian* names which translate some- thing like *talks too much, man of many gifts, he who has many strings attached* or *the nervous one who builds roads.*

While many white politicians may look forward to being adopted as a colorful *indian*, there have been no offers to become honorary black people with adopted names. The white man has never been able to put together a colorful invention of black people.

In return one would expect the *oshki anishinabe* to be made honorary white people in the humanitarian games of identity, but as everyone knows, the *anishinabe* of the past have not been adopted as white brothers. The *anishinabe* were given white names by missionaries and government officials, but they have never been made honorary white people, nor has the dominant society very often permitted a person with dark skin to be an honorary anything.

The honorary *indian* game is played on both sides of the politics of race. White politicians like to know *indians* if they are interested in humanitarian imagery, and *oshki anishinabe* politicians need to know white politicians if they are to maintain the credibility of being a tribal mediator securing more federal funds for the reservation. Somewhere out of range of media cameras, the *oshki anishinabe* leaders eat fried bread and wild rice and laugh with friends about those double-crossing white politicians who are still exploiting the land, and the white politician in turn hangs his peace pipe and headdress on his office wall and drinks brandy in exclusive clubs after a heavy day of subcommittee hearings on poverty and race.

After all the games of the politics of race come more hearings and more statutes and more money and repeated promises for peace and a better life. But the poor *oshki anishinabe* wonder why the games have lasted so long and why after all the honorary rhetoric there are still no jobs, inadequate housing and facilities for health and education, and why there is still paternalistic institutionalized racism in the dominant society.

There are always new elections and renewed hopes and just enough change on the reservation to believe in the political slogans of progress without fear of losing more land. Everything takes time and the people endure the games of politicians. The people have played the game so long under the colonial administration of the Bureau of *indian* Affairs that many *oshki anishinabe* are unwilling or afraid to change the games.

In the tribal past the traditional system of tribal political authority was the family. An *anishinabe* man of experience and good judgment made decisions for himself and his family and anyone else who trusted his perception and insight. There were no elected officials making decisions for all the people. The basic political unit was the family.

Today tribal politics function in the democratic structures of elections. The Bureau of *indian* Affairs influenced the structures of tribal constitutions after the traditional family tribal sanctions were suppressed. Elected tribal politicians still reflect the pressure and influence of white specialists in *indian* affairs.

On most reservations there is no functioning economic system through which social and political experience can be shared. The people on reservations live under a colonial system reflecting the ideal political values of white men, but with no functioning independent economic system. Elected tribal politicians therefore must spend much of their time relating to white people and government officials who represent the colonial economic system. Every now and then someone young tries to change the paternalistic game.

William Lawrence tried to change the game by running for the position of tribal chairman of the Red Lake Reservation. He carried on a door-to-door campaign, talking with the people about the need for change, but he lost the election to the incumbent chairman, who had been in power for twelve years.

Lawrence was born on the Red Lake Reservation, graduated from Bemidji State College with a degree in business administration, served as an officer in the Marine Corps and is a graduate of the University of North Dakota Law School. He lives in a new house near Bemidji with his wife and two daughters.

When Lawrence graduated from high school—he earned athletic letters in three sports—he received an athletic scholarship to the University of Minnesota but interrupted college for one year to play professional baseball. After serving ten months in Vietnam as an officer, he returned to law school but interrupted his studies again to become the industrial development specialist for the Red Lake Reservation.

Lawrence developed an impressive and ambitious five-year economic and industrial development plan for the reservation, ranging from private enterprise to a tribally owned liquor store, golf course, airport, motel, fuel oil distributor and water and power companies.

In the short time Lawrence was on the job—less than a year—he had obtained federal funds to establish a bulk fuel oil dealership, an industrial park on the reservation, improvements in telephone services and communications, reforestation programs, construction of a utility building and home construction.

Lawrence was also responsible for assisting an individual in obtaining a small business loan from the federal government to build a coin-operated automatic laundry. For the first time, there is now a laundromat on the reservation. Before, the people had to drive about thirty miles to do their wash.

The long-range programs Lawrence had planned were a supermarket, motel and restaurants—visitors have no public place to stay on the reservation—service station with repair facilities, an automobile dealership and other private service businesses owned and operated by *oshki anishinabe* living on the reservation.

The economic philosophy behind his five-year plan was to establish *oshki anishinabe*-owned services on the reservation, creating an economic system independent of the federal government. Lawrence is critical of the fact that most *oshki anishinabe* on the reservation are employed by the federal government and they spend their money either in white-owned businesses on the reservation or in nearby white communities. He wanted the people to earn their money *on* and spend it *on* the reservation. He is motivated to reduce the dependency the people have on the taxpayers through federal funds, and to eliminate the control of jobs by tribal officials.

Roger Jourdain, who was elected to his fourth term when he defeated Lawrence, has many contacts and friends in federal offices. He moves around the country on a first-name basis with several national politicians. Through his political friends he was able to design and obtain federal funds for a gigantic furniture factory on the reservation which would have solved in one sweep the total unemployment problem—assuming everyone wanted to assemble furniture parts five days a week.

It was true that the plant would have solved the unemployment problem—there are about three hundred men unemployed at Red Lake Reservation—but Lawrence and at least one member of the tribal council, Francis Brun, openly opposed the operation because it was not feasible to run such a large operation without basic services existing on the reservation. That large a plant would have given the tribal council too much power over too many jobs.

The plant would have produced the furniture parts with local timber cut on the reservation and shipped by truck to other parts of the country for assembly. The feasibility of the proposed furniture plant was questioned and the project finally scrapped.

Jourdain has power and he knows how to use it to stay in power. In no uncertain terms he fights to win and he holds the record on the reservation for naming the most white people honorary *indians*. He puts on many people, laughs hard and travels to hundreds of conferences on employment, education, politics and economic development. He speaks the *anishinabe* language and gets the federal money he wants when he wants it. The withdrawal of funds for the proposed furniture plant was one of his first defeats.

Jourdain was seriously challenged in an earlier election for tribal chairman by another young man, Lee Cook, who was also born on the Red Lake Reservation and who wanted to return to the reservation as tribal chairman. He has spent most of his life away from the reservation attending college and working. He was also defeated after a door-to-door campaign. The issues in that election were about the same. Cook, like Lawrence, wanted to move aggressively for independent economic development to reduce the dependency on the federal government. The people were not ready to change.

In tribal elections there are no party lines nor a clear division of political factions. The arguments and challenges are usually between the old and the new and the young and the old. Lawrence and Cook were the new and the young, and Jourdain has been elected four times as the old and traditional.

In an article for the *Minneapolis Tribune*, a journalist described the election as a "contest between those who have stayed on the sprawling communally held reservation and those who have left to seek their fortunes in white urban society."

So far two young *oshki anishinabe* men who have left the reservation for education and employment have not been elected to return.

Other differences between the young and the old are tribal traditions and the ability to speak the *anishinabe* language. Jourdain speaks *anishinabe* and spends many hours with the old people on the reservation talking in the visual memories of the past. The *anishinabe* language is often spoken during official sessions of the tribal council.

Neither Cook nor Lawrence speaks the language, but they do understand the concepts of *anishinabe* speech. They have spent most of their lives off the reservation but return several times a year to visit relatives and friends.

Facing the challenges of two young *oshki anishinabe* college-educated men in two consecutive elections, Jourdain expressed the fear that if leadership on the reservation fell into the hands of people living in the dominant society, it would mean "termination." The word termination frightens reservation people because it has come to mean that the people living on the reservation would lose their land. But what it also means is a reduction of dependency on the federal government for services and programs.

"I would like to use my education and return to the reservation to help my people cope with the twentieth-century problems," Lee Cook said when he was a candidate for tribal chairman. He lost.

Aggressive and fast-moving, Cook is so filled with energy and excitement that his words tumble over each other when he is talking about things that can and must be done to improve the quality of life on the reservation.

He attended a parochial school on the reservation and graduated from high school and college at St. John's University in Collegeville, Minnesota. He completed an advanced degree in social work and community organization at the University of Minnesota graduate school.

Since graduating, he has been working in economic and educational programs in urban centers and on the reservation.

Cook was orphaned when he was seven years old

and was raised by his aunt, who lives on the reservation. He works with his people, he said, because "*indians* are better people and have a better outlook on life. . . . When I was young I had a chip on my shoulder to work against because I was orphaned and never had much support to make it in the world.

"But I knew I could make it on my own," he said in rapid speech, pacing back and forth and using his hands to emphasize certain points. "Athletics was not really a driving force for me. . . . I was always praised as an *indian* and being an *indian* never worked against me. . . .

"So, you see, I simply enjoy being an *indian*," he said, lighting a cigarette.

Cook has extensive experience in programs on the reservation and in urban centers, but he is drawn more to the energy of urban center *oshki anishinabe* leaders than traditional reservation leaders.

"The urban center is the best access to change in economic and political life," Cook said, punctuating his tumbling words with short breaths. "Urban organizations in the past were mostly social and cultural things, but the militants have changed that, and there have not been the problems of traditional politics that exist on the reservation."

When Lawrence filed for the office of tribal chairman, he said in a press release that he decided to become a candidate for the office "so that the Red Lake people will have a clear choice between the dictatorial and irresponsible leadership that presently exists, and leadership that would frugally and conscientiously manage tribal affairs and be responsive to the people's needs . . . the people of the reservation deserve a better fate than we are now enduring.

"My candidacy also represents an awakening of the Red Lake people to an urgent need for a change and a desire to determine our destiny, if we the Red Lake *indians* are to take our place and share equally in this society. . . ."

Lawrence emphasized again the need of the *oshki anishinabe* to trust the energy and counsel of the younger college-educated people as well as the older tribal members on the reservation.

"The potential of the Red Lake people has been ignored and lain stagnant for too long, and I believe that imaginative, progressive and unselfish leadership can be the catalyst that ignites this great people."

The *oshki anishinabe* are cautious and conservative about change because in the past it has been the promise of change by white people that has reduced the amount of land the people now own. The promises have hurt so much that the people often feel better with what they have than with taking a chance on change.

"The people are afraid of change," Lawrence said. "They know most of the time what they can expect from Jourdain." The young college-educated *oshki anishinabe* who are committed to working for a better life with good conscience must face the evil memories of what the white man has done to the people on reservations.

It was a good test of tribal leadership, and Cook and Lawrence are not through arguing and challenging what they believe must be done to improve the quality of life on the reservation. They may never run in another election but they will be working for the people. And when the next election for tribal chairman is held on the Red Lake Reservation, the challengers, and the incumbent, will be older and the voters will be younger.

The six other *anishinabe* reservations in the state are under state civil and criminal jurisdiction and have independent tribal governments which are called Reservation Business Committees. Each of the six reservations—White Earth, Leech Lake, Nett Lake, Fond du Lac, Mille Lacs and Grand Portage—elects local tribal officials to administer local tribal business. Two elected representatives from each of the six reservations—the chairman and the secretary-treasurer—form the state-wide Minnesota *chippewa* Tribal Executive Committee, which governs programs on those six *anishinabe* reservations in the state. (The Red Lake Reservation is independent of this organization.)

On each reservation there are elections for the chairman and secretary-treasurer and several district representatives from the various communities on the reservations. The twelve members of the Tribal Executive Committee elect a chairman from among the members.

Oshki anishinabe enrolled in the tribe but living off the reservation can vote by absentee ballot in all tribal elections. When Cook and Lawrence opposed Jourdain in the election for tribal chairman, both challenging candidates received substantial support from the *oshki anishinabe* living off the reservation and voting by absentee ballot. Cook concentrated on absentee voters living in the city.

Making it back to the reservation through an election seems more difficult than making it off the reservation in the dominant society.

8

What the People
Believe Is True

... evidence can be adduced to prove that force has
tended to brutalize rather than ennoble. . . . The more a
man is treated as a brother, the less demand for law.
The less law there is, the more will man be honoured. . . .

—George Copway, *anishinabe* missionary, 1850

An *oshki anishinabe* youth was helping his friends
push a car out of a driveway in the city when a young
policeman approached with his revolver drawn and
told the youths to line up against the wall of a building.

Three *oshki anishinabe* youths leaned against the
brick wall with their hands raised in submissive fear of
the police officer who questioned their identity.

"Who are you . . . what are you doing here. . . ."

They were the sons of the *noble savages* who
roamed the woodland, the people whom white people
envy in inventions and place wooden effigies of in

front of cigar stores, and name streets, and parks, and lakes after . . . they were sons of the *anishinabe* heroes in the wars of the white men.

One youth standing near the end of the building lowered his hands slowly and then ran down the street. He was driven by fear. A few seconds later he stumbled face forward into the street with a bullet hole in his head. He was dead.

The automobile had *not* been stolen. The three *oshki anishinabe* youths were only pushing it out of a driveway because it would not start. The youths were frightened, as every *oshki anishinabe* is, of the police in the city. Carrying out his duty, the policeman took a life—and then he found out no crime had been committed.

The death of the *oshki anishinabe* youth was ruled justifiable and the police officer was officially exonerated from any wrongdoing. The protectors of the dominant white society have seldom been guilty of any wrongdoing, but the death of the youth was genocide in the memory of the *anishinabe* community.

For weeks the people gathered on the streets and in their homes in the city to talk in hushed voices about the brutality of the police. Stories were compared about other police incidents the people remembered— beatings in dark alleyways by the blue-uniformed protectors who remove their badges or cover them with their hands to avoid identification. The people remember violent thrusts from nightsticks in police cars and in the jail elevator after being arrested.

For years municipal court judges have seen the battered faces and heads of the *oshki anishinabe* in court. Little has been said and even less has been done to understand the racial hostility of policemen. The police would say the marks of clubs and abrasions from tight handcuffs were self-inflicted by the accused or sustained in falls and street fights. Sitting next to the *oshki anishinabe* in court all these years were white men who had been arrested—but few white men bear such marks.

When legal complaints were made through human and civil rights organizations to police officials, they would demand badge numbers, dates and witnesses, and other information that someone on the other end of a nightstick would have little thought in gathering. The most protection the people need is protection from the police.

"Why must the *oshki anishinabe* bear the burden of policing the police . . . a citizen has a right to expect justice," an *oshki anishinabe* leader told police officials in a meeting about police harassment.

But, the police officials explained, while there *may* be a few men on the force who have prejudicial thoughts, we need specific information. In the few cases the police department has been given *specific* information nothing has happened.

"Then forget the facts and believe what the *oshki anishinabe* say—" the leader said, "begin with what the people believe is true."

The polarization between the *oshki anishinabe* and

the police is so great that when a federal manpower training program was seeking people to participate in a training program to become police officers, no *oshki anishinabe* expressed interest. The way the people feel about police is best expressed in the fact that no one could be found to accept free training to become a police officer.

Police hostility and harassment are not problems limited to the urban center. The problem is even more serious, but less often obvious, in white communities near the reservations. The six *anishinabe* reservations in the state are under state civil and criminal jurisdiction and have as their law-enforcement officer the county sheriff. This means that people arrested on the reservation must spend the night in jail in a white community off the reservation. Many county officials resent the burden of jursidiction on the reservation, which is tax-free land.

The *oshki anishinabe* can tell thousands of stories of police brutality and harassment. As in the past the dominant society exonerates and leaves a good record. White men have also excluded from history the brutality toward the *anishinabe* in the past. The dominant society has a good record and the *oshki anishinabe* have a good memory. What the people believe is true. The facts are no longer important.

There are always men who mitigate the harsh realities of life by their attitudes of humanity and justice. One such man was *oshki anishinabe* Ira Isham, who was the county deputy sheriff on the Nett Lake

Reservation, where he was born. He was a dedicated man with more than punitive interests in his community.

Isham lived on the same reservation where he enforced the law, but the law under Isham was more than a book of offenses designed by the dominant society. The law was to protect people.

A veteran of combat in the South Pacific during World War II, Isham was a law-enforcement officer for more than fifteen years.

Isham knew the people and he knew the language. There was a basis for mutual respect. He often enforced what he called *customary law*; rather than an instant arrest with a tell-it-to-the-judge attitude, Isham worked out the problem where it happened.

He was reluctant to arrest *oshki anishinabe* unless a serious crime had been committed because, he once explained, he did not like the idea of taking a person from the reservation to jail or any other institution in the white community. This does not mean that deputy Isham overlooked criminal behavior, particularly in serious crimes against the person, but in minor offenses involving property or public disturbances, he was respected for resolving the problem on the reservation without a dehumanizing night in jail.

When possible, Isham would enforce *restitutive* rather than *retributive* justice on the reservation when a crime involved property.

He told the story about an *oshki anishinabe* youth who stole a motorcycle from a white man on the

reservation and then out of fear abandoned the vehi-
cle. The motorcycle was found and returned to the
white man but it had been damaged. Isham
approached the youth, whom he had known for many
years, and offered persuasive evidence of his guilt in
the theft, but suggested the youth voluntarily agree to
pay for the repairs of the damaged motorcycle.

The next day the youth spoke to the white man and
the matter was settled. Isham was pleased with the
way things turned out, he said, because the white man
has a better feeling about the reservation and the
people, and the youth will not have to be burdened
with the guilt of the theft or, worse, with an arrest and
conviction for the crime.

While on duty Isham suffered a heart attack and
died. More than a hundred white law-enforcement
officers from all over the state attended the funeral on
the reservation honoring *oshki anishinabe* deputy
sheriff Ira Isham. He was a respected man in two
worlds.

The Red Lake Reservation is the only reservation in
the state which has never been ceded to the federal
government as trust land. Residents of Red Lake have
original title to the land. Nor have federal land
allotments been made on the reservation, which means
that the reservation was excluded from federal legislation transferring civil and criminal jurisdiction to the
state government.

On the Red Lake Reservation the people have their
own constitution and tribal courts and law enforce-

ment officers handling minor civil and criminal offenses. Major crimes committed on the reservation, such as murder and grand larceny, are under the jurisdiction of federal courts.

In a research paper titled "The Legal System of the Red Lake Reservation" that William Lawrence wrote as partial fulfillment for his degree in law, he compared the tribal legal system on the reservation to the modern legal systems of today:

"Traditional *indian* law stressed *restitutive* rather than *retributive* justice in criminal cases. In the classic example of murder, instead of merely being punished, the [offender] was required to support the family of the victim."

About the tribal judges on the reservation Lawrence writes: "The judges are, as a rule, tribal members with little or no legal training, thus making them heavily dependent upon the superintendent [an official of the Bureau of *indian* Affairs on the reservation] for direction. Equally disturbing is the fact that reservation law enforcement is also under the authority of the agency superintendent. Thus with complete control over the law and order system, one individual is able to unduly influence the life and property of a sizable group of people. . . .

"The Red Lake Court of *indian* Offenses specifically established to render justice to tribal members equally is probably little more than a kangaroo court. . . .

"It appears quite evident that the Red Lake Court of *indian* Offenses, like other tribal courts, would be in jeopardy if it were made to stand the test of due process. . . ."

The constitution of the Red Lake Reservation specifically prohibits the possession of alcoholic beverages on the reservation, but crimes associated with drinking constitute, Lawrence explains, most of the criminal charges involving the *oshki anishinabe* on the reservation:

"Reservation prohibition not only has been ineffective in preventing access to alcohol, but it has contributed to the problem. As with national Prohibition there is widespread disrespect for the law, an unwillingness on the part of reservation officials to enforce it, easy access to bootleg liquor, and development of groups economically interested in retention of the law. . . ."

Lawrence continues that it is "ludicrous to consider that the only legal way in which a tribal member can bring liquor on the reservation is in his stomach. The necessity of consuming a purchase before returning to the reservation contributes to the incidents of drunkenness, as well as that of driving while intoxicated. . . ."

Residents of the reservation who wished to legally purchase strong beer or hard liquor must drive at least twenty-five miles to the nearest white community. One white community near the reservation supports the town government through the proceeds from a municipal liquor store.

Lawrence has proposed that the tribal council offer a referendum repealing the constitutional prohibition of liquor on the reservation and establish a tribally owned liquor store.

"Permitting alcohol on the reservation," Lawrence writes, "is unlikely to worsen conditions and might even facilitate a move toward more responsible drinking . . . the band [tribal members of the Red Lake Reservation] would benefit economically if funds now spent for alcohol could be so used on the reservation; not only might taxes be levied upon such sales, but the profits would be retained within the band, particularly if a tribally owned package store were established."

Lawrence is committed as a student of the law to the constitution and as an *oshki anishinabe* he is committed to improving the quality of life and government on the reservation. He is a reformer and idealist who will not easily tire of demanding responsibility and fairness in government and law enforcement on the reservation.

"For reservation *indians*," he writes, "tribal sovereignty is not an abstract concept, a cultural relic, or even a vanishing institution. On the reservation the tribe represents to its members not only the local government, but also a dominant force in their economic and social lives. These powers include the authority to define conditions of tribal members, to regulate domestic relations of members, to prescribe rules of inheritance, to levy taxes, to regulate property within the jurisdiction of the tribe, to control the conduct of members by tribal legislation, to administer justice, and to determine allocation of communally-owned wealth.

"Thus the tribal government exercises the most important governmental power for most reservation *indians*. Tribal governmental actions have sometimes exceeded constitutional limits imposed on state and federal governments. Some of these departures can be attributed to the lack of finances and education that would be necessary to meet constitutional standards.

"When the Senate Subcommittee on Constitutional Rights discovered that reservation *indians* are not accorded the same rights, privileges and immunities by their tribal government as required of the state and federal government, their reaction was not whether to act, but rather how far and fast to proceed. . . ."

The problem of tribal actions in the enforcement of the law on reservations, and the jurisdiction of state and federal governments, is not experienced by the *oshki anishinabe* living in the city. They demand that the existing system of justice in the white courts be as fair and equal to the *oshki anishinabe* as to the members of the dominant society.

Harold Goodsky, who was born on the Nett Lake Reservation, is employed as a probation officer by the county court services in the city. He works exclusively with *oshki anishinabe* young people in trouble with the law.

After two years on the job, Goodsky feels that the courts are a "closed book and I don't know if the book will ever open up to *indians*.

"I once had the belief that I could teach white

people about *indian* feelings, and adapt *indians* to white courts, and help the white understand the problems . . . but I don't really think I can be effective, because I sort of walk down the middle between the whites and my people.

"The *indians* call me a sell-out," he said, almost whispering, with his arms stretched out across the dining room table in his two-bedroom apartment, "but I believe in what I am doing . . . and the white people say I am hiding behind the bag of being an *indian*."

The beads of perspiration grew on his arms as he talked. It was a hot summer night in the city. Goodsky had spent a long day in the community talking with young people on probation. His sensitive attitude and style keep him present in the community with his people but not watching them or looking for things they are doing wrong.

"My people need somebody on their side, and that's why the court needs me," he emphasized, clenching his fist. "They need me to tell the court that what the people are saying is not untrue. These people in the court have never visited a reservation and they don't know what a hard life is all about."

Until Goodsky joined the navy he had not left the reservation of his birth. He believes in *anishinabe* religion and speaks the language of the people. On an impulse he will often drive back to the reservation just to talk with friends and relatives in the *anishinabe* language.

He came to the city to live when he was discharged

from the service. His parents still live on the reservation.

Goodsky has a high school diploma and worked as a construction laborer before he became active in *oshki anishinabe* youth organizations in the city. He has continued his interest in youth organizations while working in the poverty program as a community organizer and is active in the militant American *indian* Movement.

"The *indian* people are tired of answering the door and finding some super-white social worker standing there to rescue you," Goodsky said with mixed humor and seriousness. "Your hard times are over, the social worker mutters, and right away he asks the same old questions, like what's your name, how many children, how old are you, how many times a week do you have sex.

"The *indian* knows everything there is to know about paperwork, and when the *indian* wants to be heard his voice is lost in the paper."

Goodsky refuses to deal in paper and is reluctant to conduct investigations for the county court services until the court understands the feelings of the people first. His brow wrinkles and his voice shifts from almost a whisper when he is serious, to head-tossing explosions of laughter when he is teasing. His humor and teasing are not always understood. For example, he demanded with all seriousness that he be given a *red* telephone for his desk because he did not want to be like all the other court workers with *white* and *black* phones.

"It's time they recognize who we are," he said through his laughter, "and a *red power* telephone is as good a place to start as any. They took me so seriously I decided to keep it that way and demand a *red* desk and *red* chair."

Because of his job in the courts he comes in contact with many white people curious to know all about the colorful traditions of the *indians*. He is often asked by white people to comment on the impression that the *anishinabe* drink too much.

"I say that the white man has been drinking for centuries on end, and the *indian* couldn't legally drink until a few years ago, so we got one hell of a lot of catching up to do. . . ."

Goodsky shares the attitude with Ira Isham that every effort should be made to keep young people out of jail and out of white institutions. Goodsky is bitter about what institutions do to the *oshki anishinabe*, but he is even more bitter about what the police and the courts do to his people. His sense of hope overcomes his bitterness and he tries again every morning.

While he verbally indicts the police for their treatment of young people on the street, he has set up a regular weekly basketball game between the police and members of the militant American *indian* Movement. Goodsky plays hard and takes exacting pleasure in defeating the police on the basketball court and out of uniform.

George Mellessey, who was born on the White Earth Reservation, has been working for the *oshki anishinabe* in the courts without salary.

Mellessey is a retired painting contractor who has lived in the city for more than thirty years. When he retired he had no problem deciding what to do with his time.

"I could have sold my home and gone back to the reservation," he said in a harsh voice, "but what good would that do me . . . what I needed was a little challenge because life is still interesting to me."

Mellessey appears in court every morning to represent any *oshki anishinabe* who needs help. He wanders from courtroom to courtroom checking with the people, asking over and over again, *what are you charged with, do you need an attorney, can you post bail, do you want me to call anyone, if you need me for anything just ask the judge.*

To the *oshki anishinabe* appearing in court, the name Mellessey is a good one. He is like a father to the young people, and the court recognizes and honors his responsibility to them. He has the authority to have people released from jail in his custody.

"I'm one of those grass-roots *indians*," he said, enjoying the use of well-worn phrases. "I don't have a degree in anything."

Mellessey attended federal boarding schools but did not graduate. He has five children and lives with his family in his own home in the city.

He helped organize and was elected chairman of the National *indian* Council on Alcohol and Drugs; he now has two jobs with no salary. The new organization is dedicated to the research and rehabilitation of *indian* alcoholics. The governing body is an all-*indian* board divided into eleven districts throughout the nation.

,Mellessey may be considered an old man to the young *oshki anishinabe* he works with, but his attitudes and compassion are youthful and aggressive.

He is firm when he tells young *oshki anishinabe* they should fight more and more for their rights as citizens. "You will receive your rights if you assert your rights," he is often heard saying.

About the stereotype of the *oshki anishinabe* as a heavy drinker, Mellessey argues that the people drink no more than white people, "but I can see where a lot of white people could have good reasons for their contention, I think, because our people have been victims of chemical warfare from the very beginning. . . ."

Whatever the frustrations and problems of working for the people through the system of white courts, the *oshki anishinabe* committed to justice in the courts will not easily give up the responsibility of serving the people. As the number of people working in the courts grows, the number of frustrations with the system will also grow, and if frustration can change anything, it will change the racist system of justice that the *oshki anishinabe* have endured for so many years.

"An *indian* in trouble not only needs a good lawyer but he needs another *indian* in the court to talk with about his feelings," said Harold Goodsky, with his forehead gathered in wrinkles, "so I could never leave my place in the courts because we may write a new chapter for the closed book about the *indian* feelings that should never be forgotten in the court. . . ."

"We have never had a voice in the making of laws," Mellessey said, "but we have to comply with them anyway in the courts of white men. . . . Our true laws come from the treaties and if we demanded our aboriginal treaty rights in court the judges would not know what to do. . . ."

9

No One Else
Can Represent
My Conscience

I will myself
test the power of my spirit

—*anishinabe* song poem

A tall *oshki anishinabe* woman walked toward the
front of the carpeted chambers to speak to the
members of the City Council. The public microphone
was shut off, so Loretta Beaulieu raised her voice and
told the members of the council that they must face
the problems of *oshki anishinabe* living in the city.

The elected president of the Minneapolis City
Council smiled politely and explained very slowly that
her remarks were not in *order*. She would not be
permitted to speak to the council while it was in
session.

Loretta Beaulieu objected and argued that she had the right and responsibility as a citizen to address a legislative body about the problems of minority people.

The council members smiled nervously while she continued to tell them that they must correct the injustices that the police and many other governmental agencies have perpetuated against the *oshki anishinabe*.

She was asked again to be silent. When she would not stop talking she was removed from the council chambers by two policemen. She protested on the way out the door that she was being denied her constitutional rights to address a legislative body elected to represent the people.

She was taken to the city jail and charged with public drunkenness. She had not been drinking.

Later that morning she was released on bail provided by an attorney who was present in the council chambers when she was removed.

"She was a perfect lady as she approached the microphone and sought to get the attention of the council and sought to speak," the attorney said under oath.

The elected representatives of the city in which more than ten thousand *oshki anishinabe* live recessed for lunch, and Loretta Beaulieu walked home on bail in the cold winter wind thinking about how she would defend herself in court.

The Minnesota American Civil Liberties Union learned of the circumstances of her arrest and sent two representatives to her home to offer legal assistance.

Sitting in an overstuffed chair in her one-bedroom apartment in the *oshki anishinabe* neighborhood of the city, she rested her chin on her hands and without hesitation refused the assistance of an attorney or any organization.

"If you have been burned as many times as I have, and my people have, you would be wary of people bearing gifts," she said, staring at the two representatives long enough to make them feel uncomfortable.

"You have not walked in my moccasins," she said, repeating a popular phrase of the people. "Only I know what this is all about and I must defend myself. No one else can represent my conscience."

Like her ancestors who learned the secrets of herbal medicine and foretold the future, Loretta Beaulieu believes she has prescient dreams and is moved by the power of a vision to defend the rights of the *oshki anishinabe.*

She dreams of a world of equality and absolute justice, where *all* the people truly rule the nation.

Everyone is an immigrant to the United States, she explains—including the *oshki anishinabe* and other tribes who were the first immigrants—and because man did not originate on this continent the people who have settled here have all built this nation. Therefore, she emphasizes, the United States belongs to the whole world because this nation was built by people from every national, religious and ethnic origin.

She believes in herself as a visionary defending the United States Constitution and leading the world toward justice. She explains that her psychic powers have influenced many people to follow her vision and dream of a united world.

"The ground is soaked with the blood of my people," she whispered in a harsh voice and then relaxed in her chair. "When I deliver the message it is important that I be a nobody with nothing. . . ."

She looked down and was silent for a few minutes and then smiled. She slapped her knee, suddenly changing her whole mood.

"Don't you know that everyone should demand a jury trial . . . the police and judges have a hard time stepping on your rights when the members of a jury are sitting there, taking everything down. . . .

"This lack of respect people have for the law is caused by the lack of respect the law has for people. . . . Let the damned law clean itself up before it starts trying to clean up the rest of us," she said, jabbing a finger in the air.

She jumped up at the end of her sentence and went into the kitchen for more coffee. When she returned her mood had changed again. She stared intensely into space through her dark-rimmed glasses.

"Don't you know that this country is the biggest mess created in the history of all mankind," she said very slowly, nodding her head. "The only thing that is going to bring order into the midst of this chaos is our common bond in our common banner, our stardom in the crown of Old Glory, the banner of the Lord . . .

She sighed and relaxed in her overstuffed chair and again she was silent. While she was sipping her coffee,

the wrinkles left her forehead. She smiled and said:
"The one thing that white people hate the most is a
smart redskin."

She would not compromise her personal philosophy
and intense conscience by accepting legal assistance
from anyone. Independently she had decided to enter
a plea of not guilty to the charge of public drunkenness
and demand a trial before a jury of her peers.

Loretta Beaulieu appeared in court a few days later.

When the judge asked her if she was represented by
counsel, she replied calmly that she was her own
counsel. She took a seat opposite the city attorney and
in front of the two policemen who had removed her
from the city council chambers.

She was denied a jury trial because state legislation
has limited the privilege of a jury trial in certain
municipal violations of the law. Denied her request,
she said she would then stand mute and not defend
herself.

"Your Honor," she asked in a lilting voice, "in the
absence of a jury of my peers, am I allowed to make
an opening statement to the court?"

The judge smiled and explained carefully that she
would be permitted to examine each witness and
object to any questions in the course of the examina-
tion of the two witnesses.

"Well, Your Honor, I have something to say in
advance which does have a bearing on this case."

The judge departed from ordinary courtroom proce-
dure and permitted her to make an opening statement
to the court.

"Now, my plea is not guilty because I am innocent, but I cannot defend myself while being deprived of my right under the Constitution of the United States to a trial by jury.

"*If obeying one law means violating another,*" she told the judge, "*I have a right to decide which I would rather have on my conscience.* In my eyes, loyalty lies with the highest law of the land—the law that no other law in the land supersedes, and I will stand by it just as I always have.

"Now," she said, pointing her finger at the judge and stretching her neck forward, "consider this, Your Honor: We *indians* became citizens of the United States on June 6, 1924, and when Repeal came for the rest of the nation in 1933 it should have come to us too.

"But it didn't come for twenty years, until 1953," she said, meaning that the *oshki anishinabe* were not legally permitted to drink until less than twenty years ago.

"But in 1946 the State of Minnesota passed a law permitting the sale of liquor to *indians*," she explained, and then paused, shuffling her feet beside the city attorney who was tapping his pencil on a yellow legal pad.

"No state law supersedes the federal law," she continued in rapid speech rhythms. "That law was in effect for two days and the bars were slamming the doors in our faces all over again.

"*So if no state law supersedes a federal law in that case, no state law supersedes a federal law in any case,*"

*including denying me the right under the Constitution
of the United States to a trial by jury.*

"So my plea is not guilty because I am innocent but
I cannot in all conscience defend myself while being
deprived of my right under the Constitution of the
United States to a trial by jury, so there will be no
defense for the reasons stated."

The city attorney stopped tapping his pencil and
leaned forward with his lips parted to watch a most
uncommon *oshki anishinabe* woman take her seat on
the other side of the table and calmly knit her hands in
her lap.

"Very well," the judge said, instructing the city
attorney to proceed with the two witnesses for the
prosecution. When the testimony of the two policemen was completed the judge asked a few simple
questions about the behavior of the accused and found
Loretta Beaulieu not guilty.

The *oshki anishinabe* who were present in the
courtroom followed her down the hall and out of the
building into the cold.

She had her day in court, and her friends remember
her saying as she left the courthouse that "the court is
the church of my faith, and I shall avenge the mockery
that has been made of the Constitution."

She has been dreaming for a long time.

10

Little More Than
an Inside Toilet

If obeying one law means violating another, I have
a right to decide which I would rather have on
my conscience. . . .

—Loretta Beaulieu, *oshki anishinabe* thinker, 1968

When the area director of the Bureau of *indian* Affairs
in Minneapolis walked into his carpeted office one
morning he found a young *oshki anishinabe* twirling in
his expensive, high-backed swivel chair.

Unaware of history, the boy twirled and twirled
until he got bored and left for a tour of other offices in
the building.

The office of the director had been seized by
members of the American *indian* Movement. They
arrived early and announced that they were staying on
the federal carpets, among the drapes and pictures of
the Presidents, until changes were made in archaic

policies controlling the lives of the people on the reservations and in the city.

The people have had thoughts about taking over the Bureau of *indian* Affairs for more than a century, but the actual plan to seize the area office in Minneapolis was organized in less than a week. Militant leaders, young and old *oshki anishinabe*, residents of the city and the reservation, and whole families were sitting in the director's office waiting for history to be changed.

The people believed their courage would change the world. In time they would learn that nothing had changed.

Wearing a beaded headband and moccasins, an *oshki anishinabe* asked the director of the area office how long he had been working for the Bureau of *indian* Affairs.

"Thirty-one years," he answered without hesitation. "And I have a very, very good reputation."

"Would you say that you have enjoyed your work and the bureau has done a good job?"

"Yes, a very good job," the director said with pride. "I have many *indian* friends."

The people groaned and then laughed, drowning out the last words of the director. They did not see themselves as *indians*, nor as his friends.

It was a bad day for the white director. He was being held responsible in one day for all the known and unknown sins that have been committed against the people by the federal government.

Time passed slowly for everyone. The excitement

was wearing thin on the faces of the militants. The area director sat at his desk attempting to discuss the demands made by the leaders of the occupation. The room was filled with smoke. The *oshki anishinabe* children were rubbing their eyes. Questions were never answered. Discussions were never completed. The telephone rang and tempers flared when the director referred to the progress the bureau had made in working with the people on the reservations.

An *oshki anishinabe* in long hair and knee-high moccasins asked how many reservation people served on the school boards of federal boarding schools.

A woman asked the director if he was a racist.

An *oshki anishinabe* child asked if he could have something to eat.

The questions were repeated.

The area director seldom answered.

Responding to a question about his salary, the director said he earned over twenty thousand dollars a year.

"Do you know how many people can eat in one year for that salary?" an *oshki anishinabe* woman yelled, wagging her finger at the director. Her husband had left her and the children on the reservation. She moved to the city and receives welfare assistance.

The telephone rang.

The militant leaders demanded that the Bureau of *indian* Affairs be restructured to serve both the urban and reservation people equally.

The leaders demanded that an immediate investiga-

tion of the bureau be conducted by an all-*indian* team
. . . *exemption of* indians *from federal and state taxes*
. . . *an appropriation of half a million dollars for urban*
indian *programs . . . turn all jobs in the bureau over to
the people . . . construct hospitals on every reservation
in the state . . . return to the people exclusive hunting
and fishing rights on the reservation.*

The director explained several times that most of
the complaints were out of his hands because the
bureau was responsible only to the people living on
reservations. He said the demands should be made to a
legislative body, not to an administrative office of the
government.

"When has the bureau ever helped the people fight
for what they want?" George Mitchell snapped.
"Why don't you people help us just once fight for
what we want?

"Everything is the reservation," Mitchell snarled.
"But this is the largest reservation right here in the
city . . . when will you help the people living here?"

The area director tired of the confrontation and
called the city police to clear the building. One police
officer arrived, and the people told him to leave
because the building belonged to the people and it was
their bureau. They were the people the offices were
staffed to assist and they were staying.

The area director took a long lunch on the first day
of the occupation, and on the second day he signed a
complaint which gave the police the authority to clear
the building.

Nine *oshki anishinabe* were carried from the building by police officers and taken to the city jail in a police van. Dennis Banks, director of the American *indian* Movement, stood in the door of the van with his arm raised and his fist clenched—the symbol of the oppressed expecting to be oppressed. The doors of the van were closed to the steady beat of a tribal drum and the voices of *oshki anishinabe* singers.

While the militants were on the way to jail the director hired a private detective agency to protect the building from the people it was established more than a century ago to assist.

For several months the private detectives sat inside the front door of the area office and questioned everyone who passed . . . *what is your name, what is your business, do you have an appointment, whom do you want to see.*

Only people with dark skin were detained and questioned at the door. The director was safe. People with white skin were not questioned. Some things never change.

"The people have a love-hate relationship with the bureau," said Ronald Libertus, who was born on the Leech Lake Reservation. "Neither can function when they depend on each other for love and hate at the same time. The whole world is going to hell and the bureau guards the door to federal services."

The militant leaders have charged the bureau with racist hiring practices, but very few *oshki anishinabe* show interest in working for the bureau. The demands were being made by urban *oshki anishinabe* and not by residents of the reservations, where the people are more dependent on the bureau. Some believe that urban people are expressing a need to be as dependent on the bureau as reservation people.

Ray Lightfoot, who was born on the Red Lake Reservation, has worked for the bureau for more than thirty years. He said the "militants always demand more jobs, but at the same time they discourage people from working for the bureau." There are about two dozen tribal people working in the area office. Most of them are women in clerical jobs.

Within a year of the occupation of the area office by militants, Lightfoot was promoted to area director. For the first time, an *oshki anishinabe* was in charge of programs on reservations in four states. But his appointment did not change bureau policies, and the militants objected again. This time they were critical of a man they had originally supported.

The American *indian* Movement was organized by Mitchell, Banks and Harold Goodsky. There are more than a thousand active members, with branches in several cities across the country. The purpose of the organization and the philosophy of militancy was best expressed in a statement by Banks on the second anniversary of the movement:

" . . . we must commit ourselves to changing the social pattern in which we have been forced to live . . . the government and churches have demoralized, dehumanized, massacred, robbed, raped, promised, made treaty after treaty, and lied to us . . . we must now destroy this political machine that man has built to prevent us from self-determination.

"We must never allow another one to be built. We must never again take a back seat to anyone . . . we must, ourselves, build machines that will prevent this —not a political-type machine—but a machine built on beliefs, self-determination, freedom from oppression, and on the difference between what is *morally right and wrong* as opposed to what is *legal and illegal.*"

One of the most enduring objectives of the movement is to work with *oshki anishinabe* young people in the community.

"If we are going to have any community action at all, it will be with the young people who are working out their identity at the same time they are working with adult leaders," said Ronald Libertus, who has helped raise funds for youth programs in the city.

Militant leaders argue that there should be a special school for the *oshki anishinabe* who have moved from the reservation to the city.

"In a struggle with his own identity," George Mitchell said, "the young *indian* must find himself before he can relate to an alien society and its institutions. Too often the relationship has been forced."

Clyde Bellecourt is seen as the most controversial militant leader ever to emerge among the *oshki anishinabe.* He is both intense and soft-spoken, a fist-clencher and affectionate, a table-banger and mitigator

—he is angry and gentle, headstrong and yielding. He is complex when he is angry and very warm and affectionate to the personal needs of others when he is not angry. Bellecourt is *oshki anishinabe,* and the people find in him everything they are themselves and dislike in others.

He was born on the White Earth Reservation and attended a parochial elementary school until he was eleven years old, when he was committed to the state training school for boys as a delinquent. He was committed for being absent from school.

The next fifteen years of his life he spent in and out of correctional institutions. While in prison on a burglary sentence, Bellecourt and another *oshki anishinabe* inmate organized a group of reservation people to discuss the meaning of culture and religion. It was then, he said, that he began to understand himself.

Bellecourt voices the bitterness of inhuman experiences not only as a person of dark skin but as a man who has been committed to a correctional institution.

"They told me I already had two strikes against me," he said about the past, while leaning against the door frame in his office. "First I was an *indian,* and second I was a convicted felon."

Some *oshki anishinabe* think the leaders of the movement are interested in little more than seeing their names in the newspaper, their faces on television, and their cars rigged with short-wave radio telephones. Some believe the militant leaders are receiving a good salary for organizing their own personal complaints. And a few *oshki anishinabe* see the militants as nothing more than opportunists who should be ignored.

But most *oshki anishinabe* support the purpose of the movement while differing at times with the tactics of the leaders. But those who have experienced the frustrations of trying for change are respectful of the energy the militants give to changing the conditions of life for the people.

A militant leader seldom has a moment of personal peace. The people need him at all times of the day, because a leader who is trusted is depended upon by those who trust him. That trust and dependency call for a total life commitment. There are no vacations and quiet evenings at home for the militant leader. And there are no retirement programs.

College-educated *oshki anishinabe* generally support the causes of the militants but are not certain confrontation is always necessary when an issue might be negotiated. But every *oshki anishinabe* leader who has worked for a few years in the institutions of the dominant society agrees that because of what the militants are doing the changes from within the structure of the dominant society are much easier and more immediate.

There is some truth in all the responses to the *oshki anishinabe* militant movement, just as there is truth in the various ways of understanding and changing the conditions which have caused the problems.

"This country is sympathetic and willing to serve

indian programs," said Lee Cook, showing his concern that there might be a backlash in the dominant society. "We don't have the numbers as a small minority to risk having the doors closed by a backlash to political militants. What we really need now are more diplomats . . .

"If the militants have used every other means to express the problem and change the quality of life for themselves first and then others," Cook continued, "then they have no other way to speak out than as militants.

"But the question is whether militancy is an experience of futility," he said, looking off and pondering the question himself.

"People would be better off on their own without the federal government . . . do your own thing instead of crying about having someone else do it for you.

"The militants think they are doing a new thing, but we did the same thing ten years ago," Cook said, pitching his hands to express a reference to time. "The cry has changed from food and clothing and shelter to politics now.

"If the militants have not lost their perspective they will see that all the crying has been done before . . . the people want a program of their own now, not a new cry every year."

Cook is a persuasive diplomat but at times he is the most militant of leaders. For two years he served the needs of the people in the city, and he has never forgotten the cockroaches zipping across sinks and hiding behind a hot water pipe that runs cold. He was no diplomat when he saw children sitting on bare mattresses close to space heaters in cold, dimly lit rooms, watching television to escape the reality of poverty. Lee Cook is a good diplomat because he was a good militant who did more acting than crying.

More than 70 per cent of the *oshki anishinabe* families living in the city live in substandard housing. They pay more for broken windows, doors without locks, broken hinges, cockroaches, leaking gas stoves, cold water, and the fear that the landlord will evict them in the middle of the winter. Every *oshki anishinabe* has either lived in or knows about the conditions of life that make the best diplomats and the best militants.

Many people in the city have been down so long they see what they have as a good life compared to the past on the reservation. For decades the dominant society has ignored the problems of poverty because the people have not complained. When militant leaders educate the poor about their poverty, the militants are often criticized by white people for creating the problem.

For more than a century the *anishinabe* have been listening to missionaries and government officials and expert anthropologists and teachers tell about the good life and the many opportunities for success in the world. But the meaning of life in the city for many *oshki anishinabe* families is little more than an inside toilet.

"The one thing you can always get from a white man is a drink," said George Mitchell with bitterness. "Someone will always buy you a drink or give you a few pennies to buy a cheap bottle of wine, but try to get some money for a program. It seems to me that the white man would like to keep the people begging for a drink."

11

Buried in a Blue Suit

Silence has so much meaning . . .

—Ted Mahto, poet and educator, 1970

In the traditional tribal past when an *anishinabe* died he was dressed in his finest buckskin clothing and buried with his knees bent toward his chest—leaving the world in the same position that he had arrived.

When John *Ka Ka Geesick* died at the age of 124, in Warroad, Minnesota—a small town near the northern border of the state—he was dressed in a blue suit and white shirt and buried in a fluffy satin-padded metal coffin.

The death of the oldest *anishinabe* man in the state —his woodland life reached beyond the organization of the state and the establishment of the reservations for his people—symbolized to some people the passing of a culture and to others the strength and perpetual spiritual energy of the *oshki anishinabe* people still living in two worlds.

Many people have forgotten the tribal ceremonies, but none of the *oshki anishinabe* people at the funeral could escape the power of the *anishinabe* spirit in the songs of the *midewiwin*—the sacred religious life of the people. The sacred songs were sung at the funeral in the *anishinabe* language.

"Our past is dying," a young *oshki anishinabe* man said in the mortuary. "The old man never wore a suit. He was a singer and used herbal medicine. You can see the tattoos on his forehead."

But the young *oshki anishinabe* who spoke of the past was also dressed in a suit and tie and so were most of the people who came to touch the body of the oldest *anishinabe* man of the tribe. His spirit was still alive in those who touched his body.

The white mortician was nervous because he had heard rumors that several medicine men from the reservation would arrive to conduct a traditional *midewiwin* ceremony. The white people in Warroad— where *Ka Ka Geesick* had lived for more than a century—knew nothing about *anishinabe* medicine and religion.

The white mortician watched an old *oshki anishinabe* lean over the coffin surrounded by the sweetness of funeral flowers and place his hands on the body of *Ka Ka Geesick*. The mortician said, in his best funereal

voice, that he was not accustomed to so much touching.

Then the old man with his hands on the body began
singing an *anishinabe* honoring song for the departing
spirit of a man who had lived a long and good life.

You could hear the steady drumbeat of the past
through the beat of the hearts while the old man sang.
The room was silent, and then in small groups the
oshki anishinabe left the mortuary, each carrying a
remembrance card with the printed face of Jesus
Christ on the cover, and the Twenty-third Psalm and
the following printed on the inside:

IN LOVING MEMORY OF

John Ka Ka Geesick

DATE OF BIRTH
May 14, 1844

DATE OF DEATH
December 6, 1968

PLACE OF SERVICE
Warroad School Gymnasium

The spelling of his name and the date of his birth
were determined by white people. *Ka Ka Geesick*
means *everlasting sky*, but according to the Oblate

missionary Frederic Baraga the phonetic transcription for *everlasting sky* is *kagige gijig.* For white people and many *oshki anishinabe* who do not speak the language, the name *Ka Ka Geesick* is much easier to pronounce.

For more than a hundred years *kagige gijig* lived along the shores of Lake of the Woods in northern Minnesota near the Canadian border. He ran a trap line until the last five years before his death.

When *kagige gijig* spoke of his birth, as his relatives remember his voice, he would tell of his age by referring to an event from the past. He once told friends that he was sixteen years old when Abraham Lincoln was elected President of the United States. Or he would say that he was an old man when his cousin Tom Lightning—who is now recognized as the oldest *oshki anishinabe* man in the state—was a little boy in the village. Lightning was ninety-four years old when *kagige gijig* was buried.

Vacationing summer tourists in the popular Lake of the Woods area can buy in any drugstore a postcard showing *kagige gijig* dressed in a blue suit, orange-and-black turkey feather headdress, with a green blanket wrapped around his shoulders.

The attire was an invention for tourists, who generally expect all *indians* to wear a colorful headdress and blanket. The color photograph of *kagige gijig* printed on the card was taken by a photographer for the Minnesota State Conservation Department. The purpose of picturing *indians* on postcards and travel brochures is an apparent effort to encourage tourism and recreation. The following legend was printed on the back of the card:

Chippewa Indian medicine man born . . . on the shore of Lake of the Woods at the site of Warroad, Minnesota. Recently celebrated his 120th birthday by official village proclamation. Medicine bag always at his side, Ka-Ka-Geesick has been part of the Warroad scene since the founding of the town.

Kagige gijig was born before the state existed and lived near the lake before the white village existed. The old man was seldom seen carrying his medicine bag around the town. He was most often seen on his trap line.

Not only are the legends of the people invented by the dominant society for recreational value, but the birth date of *kagige gijig* was also invented. The Warroad Village Council selected May 14, 1844, as the official birth date of the old man. *Kagige gijig* lived in peace among the white people in the community and did not object to the invented names and legends of the past. It was important to the white citizens of the village that the old man have a birthday to celebrate each year.

And it was important to the white citizens that the old *medicine man* have a Christian funeral service and burial in the same blue suit he wore for the photograph on the postcard.

A businessman and former mayor of the village, who had known *kagige gijig* for more than twenty years, said, "It seemed that everyone knew him as an old man. When we were young he was an old man— hard to believe that when I was a young man he was almost a century old."

The businessmen in the village speak well of the old trapper who lived on a hundred-acre land allotment on Muskeg Bay in Lake of the Woods.

"About twenty-five years ago he broke his leg while he was on his trap line and it never healed right," a white man said. "When we had fresh snow you could always tell where he walked because one footprint was turned in."

"He came in to buy traps and sometimes to borrow money," another businessman said, "but he always paid it back— he was different from the other *indians*."

The last four years of his life *kagige gijig* lived in a nursing home in the village. He had practiced herbal medicine all his life. The medical doctor in the village, who often visited *kagige gijig* to learn about herbal medicine, said the old man told him the night before his death that he would live only one more night.

"He knew when he was going to die," the doctor said. The day before his death, the old man chanted several *midewiwin* songs.

Most of the businesses in the village were closed on the day of the funeral.

The *midewiwin* leader Daniel Raincloud, from Ponemah, an *anishinabe* village on the Red Lake Reservation, arrived to conduct the traditional honoring ceremony for a fellow member of the *midewiwin*.

While Raincloud and more than a hundred *oshki anishinabe* people gathered for the *midewiwin* ceremony, the white people waited outside. They were talking in hushed voices about the spiritual power of the old *indian* medicine. They were welcome, but none of the white people entered the gymnasium during the *midewiwin* ceremony. They waited for more than an hour until the traditional Christian service began, then they entered.

"What does he have in that bundle?" a white man asked, peering through the crack in the door.

"I really never thought there were any medicine men left," a white woman said.

In the middle of the gymnasium floor Raincloud and two other *oshki anishinabe* men were sitting next to the coffin. Raincloud shook a small rattle, and the three men began to sing honoring songs over the small bundle on the floor.

The sound of the rattle became a soft rustling echo like the sound of leaves on the wind between the low nasal chanting of the singers.

> *wa hi hi hi hi*
> *wa hi hi hi hi*
> brave warriors
> where have you gone
> *ho kwi ho ho*

Raincloud then approached the open coffin and spoke in *anishinabe* to the spirit of *kagige gijig*, wishing him a safe journey to the land of the spirits. He then placed a pair of red cotton gloves and some tobacco in the coffin.

The three men of the *midewiwin* then opened the bundle which contained small sandwiches for the funeral feast and packages of cigarettes. Raincloud pointed in the six directions and passed out the sandwiches to the people seated in front of *kagige gijig*. The people shared the tobacco with the soaring spirit for the last time.

The coffin was then closed and the oldest man of the tribe with his temples marked with tattoos was turned around and around on the platform to free his spirit into the layers of the next world.

"Now I am the last of the old singers," an *oshki anishinabe* man said, with his hand reaching out.

The *midewiwin* ceremony had ended, and the doors to the gymnasium were opened and the space was filled with the rhythms of a processional hymn being played on the organ. For the white people honoring the passage of the old man, Christian hymns replaced the *midewiwin* burial songs. A white Evangelical minister delivered a passionate eulogy of a man he had never seen inside his church, nor had the minister been present during the *midewiwin* ceremonies.

The village medical doctor, the mayor and two former mayors and two prominent businessmen were the pallbearers. The honorary pallbearers were the cousins and grandnephews of *kagige gijig*. The old man was buried next to his brother *Na May Puk* and *Little Thunder* in the Highland Park Cemetery.

Standing in the fresh snow at the grave you could feel the waves of heat trailing from the fires that had thawed the ground for the grave. You could hear the gravediggers talking as they back-filled the hole before the fresh earth was frozen again.

"All the *indians* are buried facing the East," one man said, between shovelfuls of steaming earth.

Index

Printed in the USA
CPSIA information can be obtained
at www.ICGtesting.com
JSHW082209140824
68134JS00014B/522

9 780873 514002